Inspired to Sew

by Bari J.

15 Pretty Projects * Sewing Secrets * Colorful Collage

stash BOOKS

Text copyright © 2011 by Bari J. Ackerman

Artwork copyright © 2011 by C&T Publishing, Inc.

Publisher: Amy Marson

Creative Director: Gailen Runge

Acquisitions Editor: Susanne Woods

Editor: Cynthia Bix

Technical Editors: Carol Zentgraf,
Amanda Siegfried, and Gailen Runge

Copyeditor/Proofreader: Wordfirm Inc.

Cover/Book Designer:
Kristy Zacharias

Production Coordinator:
Kirstie L. Pettersen

Production Editor:
Alice Mace Nakanishi

Illustrator: Wendy Mathson

Photography by Christina Carty-Francis and Diane Pedersen of
C&T Publishing, Inc., unless otherwise noted

Published by Stash Books, an imprint of C&T Publishing, Inc., P.O. Box
1456, Lafayette, CA 94549.

Library of Congress Cataloging-in-Publication Data

Ackerman, Bari J.

 Inspired to sew by Bari J. : 15 pretty projects, sewing secrets, colorful
collage / Bari J. Ackerman.

   p. cm.

 ISBN 978-1-60705-011-7 (soft cover)

1. Machine sewing. 2. Handicraft. I. Title.

 TT713.A255 2011

 646.2'044--dc22

                                            2010019010

Printed in China

10 9 8 7 6 5 4 3 2 1

contents

Lovingly Dedicated

As I create, memories of Grandpa Danny float by at the most unexpected of moments. From the very first time I sheared through fabric and began to sew, it seemed he was right there with me, watching and cheering me on. As a furrier and an artist, he was an ever-present creative spirit in my life. Though no longer physically with us, he is still present to this day.

Grandpa, this is for you. Thank you for the rides to the moon, trips to the pumpkin patch, holiday windows on State Street, and most of all, for being you.

ACKNOWLEDGMENTS

Friendship and sewing go hand in hand in my life. Without the help of my good friends at our local quilt store, Wooden Gate Quilts (formerly Quilter's Inn) in Danville, California, I have no doubt I would not be doing what I am today. Thank you, Jane, Marby, and Kathy, for not telling me how ugly that first handbag was but rather gently guiding me in the right direction.

Hugs to all of the ladies in the Monday and Tuesday sewing drop-ins, and extra big hugs to my mentors and friends Janis Stob and Margaret Lindermann, who adeptly guide us all.

I have to add an additional word about Janis. Each time I had something to troubleshoot while writing this book, she helped me work it out. Over the years, Janis has taught me so well that when I ask a question, I can nearly predict what she will say. A teacher who gives you that extra push to come up with the answer—well, that is a teacher. I can't thank her enough.

Thank you also to Mickey Krueger and Laura Jaquinto of Windham Fabrics, Kathy Miller of Michael Miller Fabrics, and Carolyn St. Clair and Lissa Alexander of Moda Fabrics for generously providing much of the fabric used in the projects for this book.

Thank you to Dan at The Sewing Machine Shop in Walnut Creek, California, for generously lending me a machine to work on when mine went kaput and was in his shop waiting sadly for its new circuit board. Thank you for getting it back to me so quickly, too.

A special thank-you to C&T's publisher, Amy Marson, and to the fabulous editors, designers, photographers, and staff who worked on this book: Gailen Runge, Cynthia Bix, Carol Zentgraf, Kristy Zacharias, Kirstie L. Pettersen, Alice Mace Nakanishi, Wendy Mathson, Christina Carty-Francis, and Diane Pedersen. And a huge shout-out and a hug to C&T's acquisitions editor, Susanne Woods, without whom I would never have dreamed of writing a book.

And thank you to my exceedingly patient husband, Kevin, and daughters, Anna and Emily, for putting up with me while I was writing this book. I love you all so much! And I'll be out of "The Sewing Cave" in just one minute!

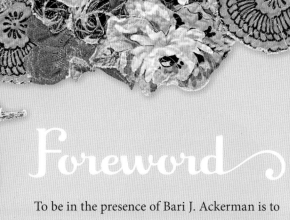

Foreword

To be in the presence of Bari J. Ackerman is to be in the presence of generosity, quality, and thoughtful attention to detail. These are the principles that exude from this most talented artist as she maneuvers through all facets of her life as a wife, mother, artist, and entrepreneur. The demeanor that Bari projects might be understated, but have no doubt—she is a creative force who knows how to set her sights on the "big picture" with the kind of focus needed to make grand gestures and lasting marks.

When I first met Bari, I could hardly believe the beauty that I saw in her handbags. The colors and textures of fabrics that her unique eye could pull together were what impressed me most. For us who love to sew, selecting the right combination of fabrics is arguably the most difficult part of the process. A primary reason Bari has become such a successful artistic sewer is her mastery of scouting luscious fabrics and combining them in fresh and fabulously unexpected ways.

Another reason for Bari's success is her ability to translate her quality fabric choices into breathtaking designs with beautiful silhouettes. This ability to do both—select fabrics and create amazing designs—is why Bari's work is so sought after and continues to gain a strong and loyal following.

This loyal following is one that I've had the pleasure of witnessing firsthand, as I have had the pleasure for many years of being Bari's editor for numerous magazine titles. Through this relationship, I have been deeply inspired with her openness to share her knowledge and teach those who want to learn. She is an artist who is passionate about sharing her tips, her tricks, and all of her wonderful techniques and design concepts. Not surprisingly, this generous approach has garnered an enthusiastic response from readers, who become entranced with her designs and her down-to-earth approach. In other words, readers love Bari's ability to keep it real.

The book you hold in your hands is 100 percent Bari. She brings you projects that you'll want to start right away. And thankfully, because she's already made them, she offers all the lessons she learned in the process—important lessons that keep things real and ensure that you are successful not only when you start but all the way until you finish.

Are you ready to be inspired? Are you ready to create? You've come to the right place, as you will find inspiration bubbling over with the turn of every page in this beautiful book filled with innovative projects presented with instructions that are easy to understand.

For real,

Jenny Doh

President of CRESCENDOh, LLC
Former Editor-in-Chief of *Somerset Studio*,
Belle Armoire & sister publications

Inspired to Sew by Bari J.

Introduction

I didn't know how much I'd love to sew. I had been at home raising my kids. Crafting was a pastime. I made jewelry from found items, collage art, and little hand-embroidered pieces, and I even sold some of these things to local boutiques.

Then I decided to give the sewing machine a whirl. It was love at first stitch.

The first thing I made was a little clutch bag with a giant felt flower brooch on it. Apparently it wasn't the prettiest sewing job on earth, but the feeling of accomplishment I had made me think it was fantastic. And I was hooked.

I kept making bag after bag, and eventually I turned all of that bag making into a successful business. I learned new techniques, experimented with beautiful fabrics, and immersed myself in this new and wonderful world of sewing I'd found.

Looking back, I realize I started sewing for the same reason I started crafting: to make interesting and original things for myself and my home. When designing, I focus on making stylish items that are artful and unique.

So when I started to write this book, I knew that would be my focus. Here you'll find projects that help you to take the reins and make your art unique—to find your own look, your own style. At the same time, complete patterns and directions allow you to get the results you want.

You'll find projects that have an art and collage feel yet are things you absolutely can wear and live with.

They allow you to be creative and individual without adding "eccentric" to the mix.

Also included in this book are features I call Keeping It Real Sewing, which are tips and mini tutorials. When I first began sewing, I was frustrated every time I made a mistake. It seemed like I never saw it coming. And I thought, "If only someone had told me that." So much was left out of some sewing patterns I was using. The pictures showed a neat and tidy ruffle being sewn on, but my ruffles were messy-looking. No one tells you that when you pull the gathering threads, the fabric frays on the edges. I thought I'd made a grievous mistake. So when I started writing my own patterns and instructions, I made up my mind to include the good, the bad, and the ugly. For that reason, throughout this book, you'll find Keeping It Real Sewing tips. I'll even throw in some embarrassing mistakes I've made. It'll make you feel really good, I promise.

The projects are made using a variety of my favorite sewing and quilting techniques. Each one is explained in a Keeping It Real Sewing mini tutorial that guides you through the steps and gives you advice. From piecing and binding to quilting, appliqué, and embroidery, these are techniques I love and skills I found I had to have.

I am so excited to be able to share with you, through this book, the joy I have found in sewing. I can't wait to see what your creativity brings to these projects. I hope you will enjoy making them your own just as much as I enjoyed creating them!

Happy sewing!

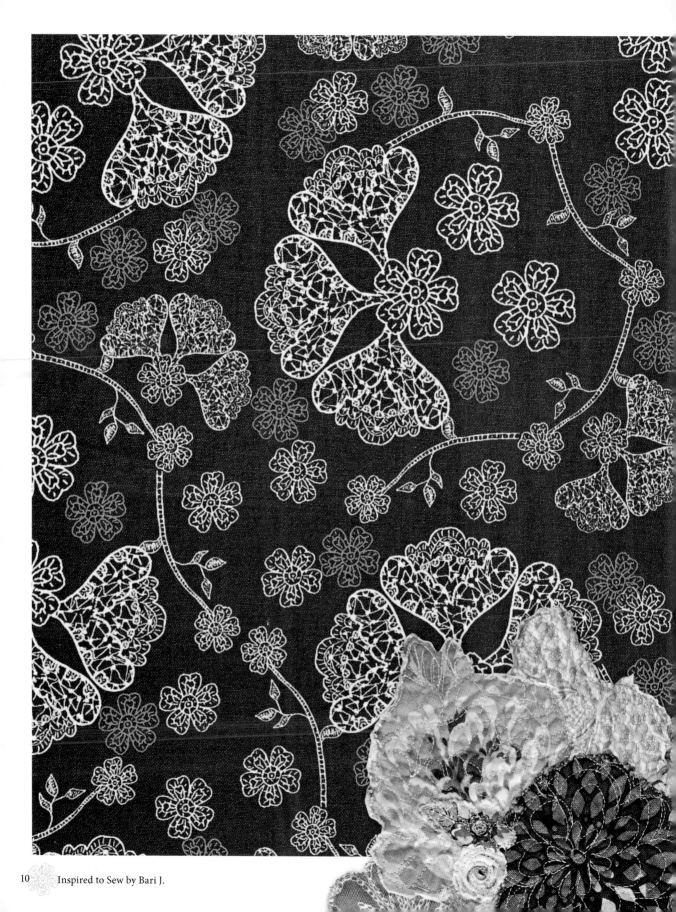

Inspired to Sew by Bari J.

Keeping It Real

This chapter focuses on sewing tools I can't do without, habits I fought learning (but am glad I did learn), and a word about fabrics. To learn where to find some of the special tools and notions, see Resources (page 126).

A few of my favorite things

Aside from the obvious scissors, needles, and sewing machine, over the years I've learned there are certain things I just can't do without in the sewing room. Every time someone asks me what I think they need, these are the things I tell them:

¼″ **sewing machine foot** | Trust me on this—you need one, especially if you are going to quilt. For years I sewed without one and wondered why things didn't come out exact. The reason was that my seams weren't exact. I know it sounds obvious, but I thought for sure I was getting it right just using the guide on my machine. Then I tried a ¼″ foot, and voilà! Perfect seams every time. I would never try to make a quilt without one again.

A lot of machine needles | I like to have a good range of these hanging around, too. I have universal needles and jeans needles, but I also like to have metallic needles around. I don't often sew with metallic thread, but for whatever reason, these sharp-tipped needles work great on collage when doing free-motion quilting, even if you're not using metallic thread.

Ruffler foot | Okay, so it's not something you can't live without, but I sure do love mine. A ruffler is a foot you can use on your machine that makes ruffles and pleats in several different lengths with ease. I can't believe how easy it is to use. I actually made the 350″ ruffle for the Sweet Home Chicago Quilt in just minutes with my ruffler! See page 119 to check it out.

Bobbins galore | I don't know about you, but I can't stand it when I run out of bobbins and I need to fill one with a new color. I keep tons of them on hand.

Seam ripper | Unsewing. Really, it's part of sewing. I don't fret anymore when I have to do it. Get a good seam ripper, and you won't either. I have one that is like a scalpel. I love this thing! Check out my resource list in the back of the book to find out where to get one. You might want to try out Alex Anderson's 4-in-1 Essential Sewing Tool, available from C&T Publishing. This tool is a seam ripper, stiletto, presser, *and* turner, all combined in a single wooden case.

Quilting rulers | These are the clear plastic rulers that come in all sorts of different sizes. I have a bunch on hand, and I don't just use them for quilting. Any time a straight line needs to be cut, I use a quilting ruler.

Rotary cutter | A rotary cutter is a cutting tool alternative to scissors that is great for cutting straight lines and cutting through multiple layers. It looks like a pizza cutter, and—well, you just have to have one. It's on top of the sewing box list for any sewer and quilter.

Small, sharp, pointy scissors | Use these for cutting threads, snipping around seam edges, and most important (to me anyway), cutting out fabric motifs … gets you around tricky corners with ease. More about that later!

Stiletto or awl | The first time I saw this on a supply list, I was baffled! A stiletto? But alas, it is not a fancy high-heeled shoe I'm talking about here. It's a sharp-pointed tool used for poking holes in fabric and leather. I use it to turn under the small edges of appliqué. It's also useful for keeping your pieces flat close to the sewing machine needle without sewing your fingertip, which isn't a pretty thing.

Freezer paper | I don't know who first realized it could be used for sewing, but this stuff is the bomb! It's great for creating pattern pieces, and the shiny side can be ironed on to fabric and then easily removed.

Woven cotton fusible interfacing | Boy, do I hate running out of this stuff. I love it fused to the wrong side of pillow fronts, bags, and pretty much anything that can use a little body.

Appliqué glue and fabric glue | These glues are used in many projects in this book. For appliqué glue, I recommend Roxanne Glue-Baste-It. For fabric glue, I like Fabri-Tac.

Double-sided fusible web | One that I use for appliqué is Wonder Under.

The good sewist

I often ignore my own good advice. But every time—without fail—I'm sorry later. Here are a few tips I've learned that have made sewing a lot easier.

Trimming threads as I go | Guilty as charged. Every once in a while, I don't trim as I go. And I end up with a mess. It's a really good practice to trim those threads before they get tangled and bothersome. It keeps your sewing neater and helps you avoid having an extra step when you are done.

Needle-down position | This is a rule I've imposed on myself that I never break. When I'm sewing long stretches, I have my machine set to stop in the needle-down position. In other words, if I stop sewing midway through, my needle automatically stays in the fabric. This helps keep lines straight and keeps fabrics from jiggling around.

Please, don't forget to close that rotary cutter! | At Wooden Gate Quilts, the local quilt shop where I go to a drop-in class each week, if you leave it open, you buy lunch. Fingers intact: good. Blood: bad. Just saying.

Pressing | We all know that pressing seams open or to one side when called for is a requirement. But I didn't realize that pressing your seams as sewn first, before you open or press them to one side, sets them in place. I did not believe it until I tried it, but it really helps the seam to look nice when you turn it, especially if it's around a curve.

Same thread in the bobbin that you use on top | I have noticed that machines tend to get a little testy about not having the same kind of thread in the bobbin as in the needle. It messes with the tension and generally creates havoc. So if you are experiencing breaking thread or tension issues, it's a good idea to make sure both threads are the same.

Skills & Techniques

I used a variety of techniques to create the projects in this book. As you'll see, I've provided short Keeping It Real Sewing sections along the way to give you step-by-step guidance in these techniques.

Collage can be used in so many different contexts. In this book it's on a pillow, a wallhanging, and a tunic. But you can collage almost anything. Try it on the edges of a quilt instead of binding or use it as decoration on a handbag. It is truly versatile.

With the ruffle how-to in this book, you are set to put a ruffle on anything you choose. Put one on a lampshade or add one to a skirt.

The techniques you learn here can be applied to projects in other books and patterns. Knowing these gives you an arsenal to work with in creative ways.

Here is a sneak peek at what you'll find.

Crazy quilting (page 88)

Top: Fabric collage with free-motion quilting (page 63)

Foolproof ruffles (page 114) and
mitered borders (page 115)

Freezer paper appliqué (page 124)

Hand embroidery (page 101)

Binding (page 81)

Inspired to Sew by Bari J.

Fabric Mixology

I'm often asked how I make decisions when mixing fabrics. My joke is that I throw it all up in the air and see where it lands. In truth, I tend to labor over what I'll put together, but I am also usually very brave in my choices. And sometimes, just when I think what I've done will never pull together—it does.

I don't have any real rules about mixing, and maybe that's why it does work out. However, I can tell you a couple of things that go through my head as I design. For starters, I think that odd pieces (the ones you'd never guess belonged together) make a design interesting. But in using those odd pieces, I do make sure they are repeated somewhere within the design. For example, the Tree of Dreams Wallhanging project (page 70) has some blue and purple velvet motifs in it. At first I wasn't so sure if that would work, but I repeated those pieces at the top and bottom of the tree, which I think pulled the design together.

Another thing that I'm sure to do in my designs is mix the scale of fabric patterns. You'll see in the Flowering Container Garden Pillow (page 65) that there is a large variety of patterns in differing scales. As I layered the pieces, if I noticed a particular section was becoming heavy in a certain color or scale, I added a varying piece.

Additionally, I really do try to step out of the box when I design. Rather than stick with fabrics that are safe and easy to put together, I tend to think I should be a little more courageous about my choices. I try to mix textures and add in unusual items—found buttons, vintage brooches, scraps of ribbon and lace. And I try to do this without fear. My motto: Thank goodness for the inventor of the seam ripper. What can be sewn can always be unsewn.

So have fun, get creative, and step out of that sewing box.

Keeping It Real
sewing basics

- Yardage listed under Materials is based on 44"/45"-wide fabric.

- Sew all seams with right sides facing, using a ¼" seam allowance, unless otherwise indicated. Backstitch at the beginning and end of all seams except darts.

- Press each seam after sewing to set it, then press it to one side.

- Keep the enclosed tear-out patterns intact. Trace onto new paper before you cut them out.

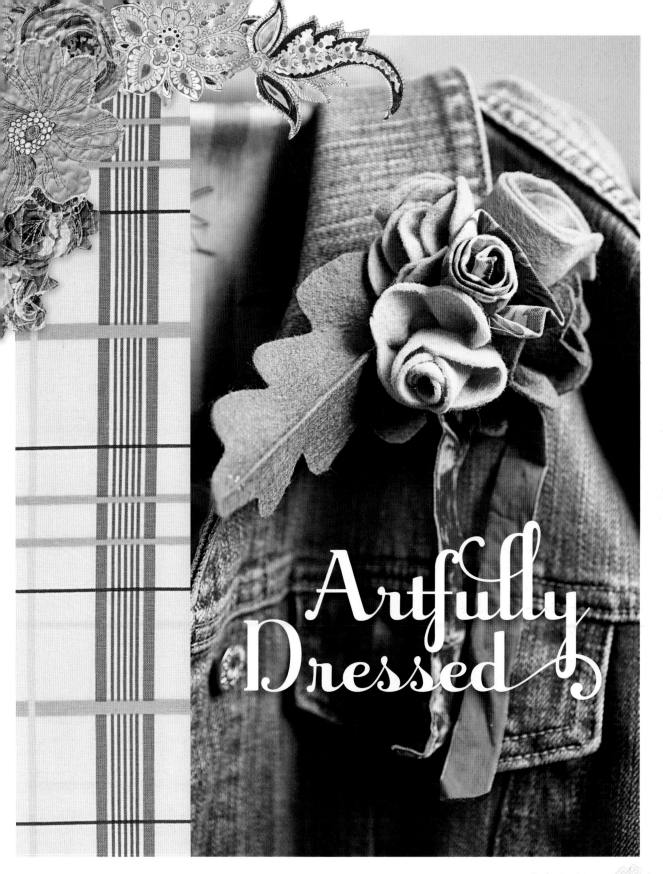

Artfully Dressed

Garden Tunic

The bias cut of the fabric and the eased shoulders of the pattern make the fit super comfy. With its floral collage neckline, this piece is highly original while still being stylish and contemporary.

This tunic is truly one of a kind.

Before you begin this project, especially if you're new to garment sewing, carefully read Keeping It Real: Garment Sewing 101 (page 29). Also see Sewing Basics on page 20.

materials

* ½ yard of small-print fabric (Fabric A) for the tunic front top

* ⅞ yard of large-print fabric (Fabric B) for the tunic front bottom and neckline facing

* 1¾ yards of small-print fabric (Fabric C) for the tunic back

* 1 yard of large-print fabric (Fabric D, or repeat Fabric B) for the sleeves

* ⅓ yard of fabric for ties, cut into 2 pieces 4″ × 38″ (This can be a different fabric or the same as one of the other fabrics.)

* 20–30 large floral motifs for the neckline collage

* 3 strips 4″ × 10″ of muslin for the collage foundation

cutting

Patterns are on pullout pages P1 and P2.

* Cut out all pattern pieces and mark notches and darts.

* Cut 1 piece 1¼″ × 35″ of Fabric B for the neckline facing.

note: Cut the pieces on the grainline as marked. Several are cut on the bias.

MAKE THE TUNIC FRONT AND BACK

1. Zigzag stitch all edges of each piece and the facing.

2. Sew the tunic back pieces together along the center seam. Press.

3. Sew the darts in the front top of the tunic as marked. Start at the bottom raw edge and backstitch. End at the bust point, and knot the threads by hand instead of backstitching. Backstitching at the bust point will cause an unattractive lump in the fabric. Press.

4. With centers matching, sew the tunic front top to the tunic front bottom. Press.

5. Sew the front to the back at the shoulder seams. Press.

Keeping It Real

Sewing Long Stretches of Fabric

This is a great trick to make sure your ends match up when you sew a long seam: Match up and pin the centers of the 2 pieces that you want to sew together. Sew from the center to an end, and then from the center to the other end.

MAKE THE TIES

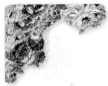

Keeping It Real

Turning Corners and Edges

It's often not easy to get the corners of pieces like these ties turned completely. I suggest poking out the corners with the end of a paintbrush and then using a pin to pull the tiniest bits out of the ends.

1. Fold each tie in half lengthwise, right sides together, and press. At an end of each tie, fold the raw edge up toward the folded edge to create a triangle.

2. Starting at the tip of the triangle, sew the fabric together as shown. Trim the excess fabric at the corner. Press, turn, and press again, teasing the seam out neatly.

FINISH AND EMBELLISH
THE NECKLINE

For fabric collage information, see Keeping It Real: Free-Motion Quilting and Fabric Collage (page 63).

ᕱ **note:** The facing you are attaching in these steps will be flipped to the inside of the tunic. The fabric collage will be on the outside.

Attach the facing

1. Starting at the point of the V, topstitch around the neckline ¼″ from the edge, backstitching at each end.

2. With right sides together, center and pin the facing to the neckline, with the excess ends of the facing at the V.

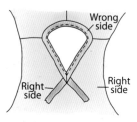

3. From the right side of the tunic, start at the V and sew the facing in place along the topstitching line. As you approach your starting point at the V, fold back the facing you left hanging at the end. Sew right up to the fold, and backstitch.

4. Clip the seam at the V right up to the stitching but not through it, and press the seam toward the facing.

5. Fold the raw edge of the facing to the wrong side of the tunic, aligning the facing edge with the stitching line, and pin in place. Press. From the right side, edgestitch the facing ⅛″ from the seam. This sews the seam allowance to the facing and makes the facing "want" to fold toward the *wrong side* of the neckline.

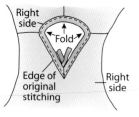

6. Press the facing to the inside along the seamline. Edgestitch close to the neckline edge, starting and ending at the V and backstitching at both ends.

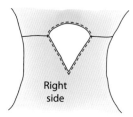

7. At the V on the inside of the tunic, trim the excess fabric ends evenly to 1″. Overlap and stitch them together (not to the tunic), sewing a square as shown.

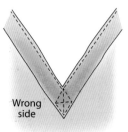

Create the neckline collage

The floral motifs should be both large and small pieces. Having varying sizes will create interest plus allow you to make the collage gradually wider toward the shoulder line.

1. Place 4″-wide strips of muslin on the neckline, overlapping into the opening. You'll need to use 3 strips: 1 for each side and 1 for the back.

2. Pin motifs artfully around the neckline. As I pinned mine on, I started narrower at the V and spread the design out as I got to the shoulder seam and the back of the tunic. Make sure all the pieces are pinned on well by giving it a shake. You don't want any pieces flipping and flopping as you quilt.

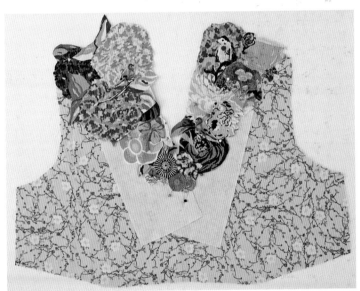

3. Using a free-motion machine foot, stitch down all of the pieces, removing the pins as you go. Be careful around the shoulder seam—it's easy to fold the fabric of the tunic in on itself and sew it together at that point. Trim off the extra muslin along both edges of the collage. Be careful not to cut into the tunic.

4. Zigzag stitch around the inside raw edge. Go 3 times around, making your stitch length shorter each time to achieve a satin-stitch effect. The outer edges will be left raw.

ATTACH THE SLEEVES

1. First, create the ease in the shoulders. When you cut out the sleeve pattern, you made 2 notches to mark the ease, notches to mark each sleeve front and back, and a notch to mark the shoulder seam. Using a basting stitch, sew from one ease notch to the other. Pull the thread to gather. With right sides together, pin the shoulder notch of each sleeve to the shoulder seam of the tunic.

2. Align the underarm edges of each sleeve with the side edges of the tunic and pin. Spread the ease evenly across the shoulder from notch to notch. Pin the whole edge in place, matching the shoulder notch to the shoulder seam, and then sew the sleeve to the tunic.

3. Turn the tunic wrong side out. Pin the tunic ties in place, with raw edges aligned above the seam between the tunic front top and bottom, keeping ties toward the inside of the tunic. With right sides facing, match the ends of the armhole seam and pin. Pin the sleeve edges together and the tunic side seam edges together.

Keeping It Real

An Easy Way to Hem

I often topstitch ¼" from the bottom edge of a piece I'm going to hem. This puts a very clear mark at the point where I will fold and press the hem, making the hem nice and even.

Keeping It Real

Pinning with Ease

To ease a seam, I find it best to first pin each end of the whole section in place. Then I pull the fabric from the end up to the notch so it is nice and flat up to the point of the ease. Do this on both the front and the back of the seam allowance. That way, the extra fabric is in the ease. Spread the ease evenly across the ease allowance.

4. Sew from the armhole seam to the bottom edge of the tunic, and then sew from the armhole seam to the end of the sleeve. Press.

note: It is important that you sew in the same direction on both sides. Doing this ensures that the flow of the fabric is the same on both sides.

FINISH

1. Press the bottom tunic edge under ¼" and then under ¼" again.

2. Topstitch on the wrong side of the tunic, ⅛" from the top of the folded edge.

3. Repeat these steps to hem the sleeves.

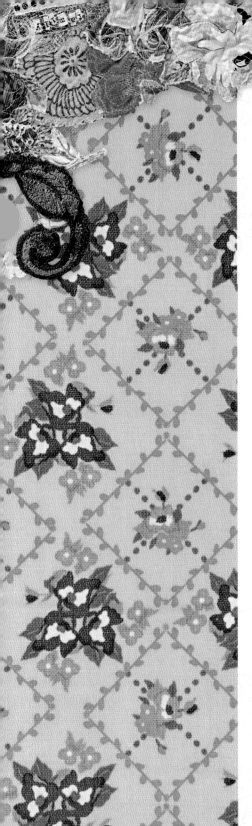

Keeping It Real

Garment Sewing 101

Looking at garment patterns can sometimes feel like trying to decode a map. There are notch and grainline marks, and lines to indicate various sizes, plus cutting instructions to figure out. Not to mention that sometimes it's hard to figure out what each pattern piece actually is. All of this may sound a bit confusing, but it's really easy to "decode" once you know what you are looking for. These are some of the basics that are used in the tunic pattern.

Pattern pieces | First things first: Figure out what the pieces are. Most patterns are marked clearly. In this pattern you will find a sleeve, a tunic back, and 2 pieces for the tunic front, all of which are marked. Figure out what size you want to make, and then cut the pieces on the heavy outer lines that are for your size.

Cutting | It's all too easy and often costly to make a mistake in cutting fabric, so read the pattern pieces carefully. Note where a grainline is marked, and align that piece with the grain of the fabric. It's especially important to do this for the tunic because it is cut on the bias. Also, note whether a pattern piece should be cut on a fold. Look to see how many of each piece to cut and whether those pieces should be cut at the same time. Often you'll be asked to cut pieces with right sides together. Sleeves are a good example of this. For the tunic, the sleeves and the back are cut this way.

Notches | Don't forget to look for notches that need to be marked before you remove the pattern piece from the fabric. These diamond-shaped markings will help you match pieces together when sewing. For example, on the tunic, notches indicate which part of the sleeve matches the front of the tunic and which goes toward the back. There are also notches that indicate where you should make a dart and where the ease is on the sleeve's shoulder.

Rags, Ruffles, and
Kerfluffles Belt

This girly, ruffled belt is easy to make and fun to wear.

I used a rhinestone buckle for a touch of glamour, but you can choose any buckle you like—new or vintage.

materials

* ⅛–¼ yard of print fabric for the belt

* ⅛ yard each of 2 contrasting fabrics for the ruffles

* ⅛ yard of fusible fleece

* Bar buckle of your choice with 1½″ opening

* Appliqué glue

cutting

* Belt fabric: Cut 3½″ wide × the length you want your belt.*

* Fusible fleece: Cut 3″ wide × the length you cut the belt fabric minus ½″.

* Ruffle fabrics: Cut several ½″ strips totaling about 4 yards in length (½-yard increments are best for creating the ruffles).

Measure your waist and add 10″—this allows 5″ for finishing the ends and folding through the buckle, plus 5″ of hangover when wearing the belt. If the measurement is greater than 44″, you'll need to piece 2 strips together.

MAKE THE BELT BASE

See Sewing Basics on page 20.

1. Center and press the fusible fleece to the wrong side of your belt fabric strip.

2. Press the short ends in ¼″ toward the wrong side of the fabric.

3. Fold the fabric in half lengthwise with right sides facing.

4. Sew the long edges together to create a tube.

5. Turn and press flat, with the seam in the center of the back.

CREATE THE RUFFLES

note: These are raw-edge ruffles.

1. Using a long basting stitch, sew straight up the center of your ½″-wide strips.

2. On each strip, pull the top threads to create a ruffle. It helps to pull from one end, ruffle the strip halfway, and then pull from the other end.

3. Press the ruffles flat with a hot iron and steam to set the ruffles in place.

ATTACH THE RUFFLES TO THE BELT

1. Mark the belt 1″ in from an end. This will be where you start the ruffles.

2. Glue each short end of 1 ruffle strip under slightly, using appliqué glue.

3. Starting at the mark, use appliqué glue to lightly tack the ruffle along an edge of the belt, aligning the ruffle and belt edges. Press the ruffle strip down.

4. Repeat with the rest of the ruffle strips until you have ruffles along both edges.

5. Stitch the center of each ruffle to the belt.

FINISH THE BELT

1. At the end of the belt where you left 1″ free, fold down the corners toward the center as shown to create a triangle. Sew across the base of the triangle, then around the tip, backstitching at each end.

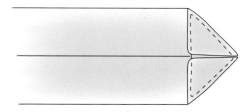

2. At the other end of the belt, slide on the buckle. Fold the end over the bar about 4″ or however long will work to size it correctly for you.

3. Sew the end to the belt to secure the buckle.

Pretty Petals
"Couture" Apron

5. On the right side of each skirt foundation panel piece, mark ¼″ from each end. You can use chalk or just a pin.

Ꮿ **note:** The foundation panel patterns are lettered C through G, starting with the top panel. Be sure to mark each piece with its letter before you set it aside and move to the next. I usually just pin on a lettered sticky note.

6. Aligning the raw edges of the petals with the top raw edge of the panel, place 1 petal at each end of Panel C on the inside of your ¼″ mark.

7. Add petals, overlapping about ½″—one over, the next under, and so on— until you have a total of 6 petals along the top edge of the panel. Baste in place, using a scant ¼″ seam allowance.

8. Repeat Steps 6 and 7 on the next 4 panels, increasing the number of petals on each panel by 1. (Panel C: 6 petals; Panel D: 7 petals; Panel E: 8 petals; Panel F: 9 petals; Panel G: 10 petals)

Assemble the panels

1. Take Panel C and flip all of the petals up to expose the bottom raw edge of the muslin panel easily.

2. Place Panel D on Panel C, right sides together, matching the bottom raw edge of Panel C with the top raw edge of Panel D. Pin in place, sew, and press.

3. Follow Steps 1 and 2 for the rest of the panels until you have all 5 panels sewn together and all seams pressed open.

CREATE THE APRON TOP AND TIES

⌒ **note:** If you haven't pieced squares for a quilt or other project before, see Keeping It Real: Perfect Patchwork Piecing (page 58).

1. Sew together the 4″ × 4″ squares in 3 rows of 4 squares each. Press.

2. Sew the rows together and press.

3. Fold each waistband tie in half lengthwise, right sides together, and press. At an end of each tie, fold the raw edge into a triangle toward the folded edge as shown. Starting at the tip of the triangle, sew along the angle, then sew the raw edges of the fabric together as shown.

4. Trim the excess fabric. Press the seam flat, turn, and press again, teasing the seam out neatly. (For a tip on turning, see Keeping It Real: Turning Corners and Edges, page 25.)

5. Repeat Steps 3 and 4 to make the 2 neck ties.

ASSEMBLE THE APRON FRONT

Now you're ready to put together the apron top, waistband, and skirt.

1. Pin, then sew the top edge of the apron skirt to a long edge of the waistband. Press the seam flat, and then press it toward the skirt.

2. Center the patchwork top on the remaining waistband edge. Pin, then sew the top and waistband together. Press the seam flat; then press it toward the waistband.

3. On the right side of the apron top, mark ¼″ in from the side edges for the neck ties. Pin the ties in place just inside the marks, matching the raw edges. Baste, using a ⅛″ seam allowance.

4. At the raw end of each waistband tie, press the center into a small pleat to fit the end of the waistband.

5. Pin the pleated ends of the waistband ties to the ends of the waistband, with raw edges even. Baste, using a ⅛″ seam allowance.

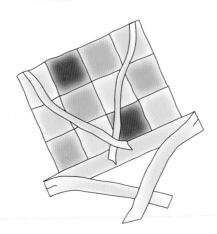

ASSEMBLE THE LINING

Repeat Steps 1 and 2 from Assemble the Apron Front (page 37) to sew together the 3 pieces of the lining: apron top, waistband, and apron skirt. Leave a 6″ opening in the center of the waistband/skirt seam to turn the apron right side out after the lining is attached.

FINISH THE APRON

1. Pin all of the petals and ties toward the inside of the apron so they are completely out of the way of your stitching.

2. Pin the apron front to the lining with right sides together. Sew, then press.

note: Make sure you feel for the edges of the petals and the ties as you sew. You want to sew as close as you can to them without going over them.

3. Turn the apron right side out through the opening in the waistband seam. Whipstitch the opening closed. Press.

Jean Jacket
Re-Vision

One of my favorite things about sewing is that it lends an aspect of creativity to every part of my life. I look at things in a way I didn't before. When I shop for clothing, I think, *This would be cuter if I changed the collar (or the pockets) or added a little something to the cuffs.*

I also realize that my old clothes can be new again … if I just think a little bit outside the box.

And the thing is, it doesn't have to be hard, either. With this jean jacket, just cutting off the bottom and rebuilding it with fun fabrics did the trick. These directions will get you started with a similar project.

materials

* Old jean jacket (mine happened to be green)
* Variety of print fabric scraps (enough to total ¼ yard of fabric)
* Print fabric strip for new bottom band and plackets
* Woven cotton fusible interfacing
* Clear quilting ruler
* Coordinating thread
* Chalk or air erasable marker

PREPARE YOUR JACKET

1. Use the quilting ruler to measure and mark 7″ up from the bottom edge of the jacket all the way around. Draw a line all the way around the jacket. Cut off the 7″-wide strip.

2. From the piece that you just removed, follow the seamlines and carefully cut off the bottom band and the button and buttonhole plackets. Set these aside; you will use them as templates later.

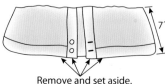

Remove and set aside.

EMBELLISH THE JACKET BOTTOM

⟡ **note:** These will be raw-edge pieces. See Sewing Basics on page 20.

1. Bring the cut jacket piece to the sewing machine with your collection of fabric scraps.

2. Starting at an end with the jacket piece right side up, place a scrap on top and stitch it down using your favorite appliqué stitch—blanket stitch, zigzag, satin stitch, or whatever. You don't have to use the same thread color throughout or even the same stitch.

3. Add piece after piece, overlapping them slightly and stitching each in place as you go, until the whole jacket piece is filled. Trim any fabric that is hanging off the edges of the jacket piece, and press.

PREPARE A NEW BOTTOM BAND AND PLACKETS

1. Measure the length and width of the bottom band that you cut off the jacket. Multiply the width by 2 and add ½″ for seam allowances to determine the width of the accent fabric strip; the length is the same as the original band. Using these dimensions, cut 1 strip each from the accent fabric and the interfacing.

2. Measure the button and buttonhole placket pieces that you removed from your cut jacket bottom. To calculate the width, multiply the width of the original piece by 2 and add ¼″ for seam allowances. For the length, add ¼″ to the length of the original strip. Using these dimensions, cut 1 strip each from the accent fabric and the interfacing for each placket.

3. Press interfacing to the wrong side of each accent fabric strip.

4. Fold the bottom band piece in half lengthwise, wrong sides together, and press.

5. Press under ¼" on one short end of each placket piece. With wrong sides together, fold each piece in half lengthwise. Edgestitch closed the folded ends on each placket piece ⅛" from the edge.

SEW ON THE NEW PIECES

1. Pin, then sew the long raw edges of the band to the bottom edge of the embellished piece. Zigzag stitch the raw edges of the seam.

2. Fold the band down and press the seam toward the band. On the right side, edgestitch the band ⅛" from the seamline.

3. Pin, then sew the raw edges of a placket piece to each end of the embellished piece with the band, aligning the hemmed placket ends with the folded edge of the band. Press the seam toward the placket. On the right side, edgestitch the placket ⅛" from the seamline.

4. Sew the embellished piece to the bottom of the jacket, aligning the front edges.

Flower Brooch

You can put one of these sweet felt brooches on anything.

They look great on a jean jacket, a handbag, or even a pillow. I used one to add extra dimension to my Seasonal Wreath (page 60).

materials

* 2 strips 10″ × 1¼″ of wool felt color 1 for the flowers

* 1 strip 10″ × 1¼″ each of wool felt colors 2 and 3 for the flowers

* 2 pieces 4″ × 4″ of wool felt in flower color 1 or 2 for the base and backing

* 1 piece 5″ × 3″ of green wool felt for the leaf

* 1 printed cotton fabric scrap at least 12″ × 3″ for 1 flower

* 2 pieces of coordinating ribbon 6″ long

* Fabric glue

* Bar-style pin (Look in the jewelry section of your craft store.)

* Pinking shears

cutting

Patterns are on pullout page P2.

From felt color 1:

* Cut 2 of pattern A for flowers.

From felt colors 2 and 3 each:

* Cut 1 of pattern A for flowers.

From print fabric:

* Cut 1 piece 3″ × 10½″ for a flower.

From the felt color for base and backing:

* Cut 1 of pattern B for the base.

* Cut 1 of pattern C for the backing, using pinking shears.

From the green felt:

* Cut 1 of pattern D for the leaf.

ASSEMBLE THE BROOCH

1. Use fabric glue to tack one end of each ribbon to base B.

2. Fold the leaf in half lengthwise. Topstitch ⅛″ from the center fold, backstitching at each end. Trim the threads.

3. Use fabric glue to tack the bottom of the leaf to base B, covering the ribbon ends.

4. Sew a basting stitch a scant ¼″ from the long straight edge of each flower strip.

5. Gather each strip by pulling a thread to ruffle it. Tie off the gathering threads and trim.

STITCH THE FLOWERS

1. To create each felt flower, roll the ruffled felt from one end, slipstitching the layers together along the bottom edge as you roll. Do *not* trim the thread ends.

2. Using the same thread, sew the flower to base B. Bring the needle up from the bottom and sew all the way around the base of the flower to hold it in place.

3. To make the fabric flower, press one short end of the fabric strip under ¼″. Fold the strip in half lengthwise and press again.

4. Follow the felt flower instructions to gather the long edges together, roll the flower, and attach it to the base. Begin the roll with the unfinished edge.

5. Once all of the flowers are secure, stitch the bar pin to backing C. Glue the backing to the back of the base.

PATCHWORK ROSE
Zippered Bag

FINISHED SIZE: 15½″ w × 9″ h × 4″ d

This one-of-a-kind bag features a patchwork of small squares turned sideways, or "on point," which gives it a unique flair. Its ribbon rosette details add a whimsical touch and are fun and simple to create, while pockets on both the back and the inside lining add modern convenience. For help with patchwork, see Keeping It Real: Perfect Patchwork Piecing (page 58).

This bag is also The Cure for Zipper Fear!

This method is super-easy and has totally cured me of zipper phobia. You'll be extra proud you did it when you are carrying this uber-cute bag, too!

materials

If desired, you can use the same fabric for the zipper placket lining and outside placket to avoid confusion when sewing.

* Various contrasting print fabrics (about 5), each at least 2½" square, to total ½ yard, for the patchwork bag front panel and outside pocket

* ½ yard of solid-color fabric for the bag back (I used denim.)

* 1 fat quarter of fabric for the bag sides

* 1 fat quarter of fabric for the bag bottom

* ¼ yard of fabric for the top (zipper placket)

* ¼ yard of fabric for the handles

* 1 yard of fabric for the lining*

* 1 yard of fusible fleece

* 1 yard of woven cotton fusible interfacing

* 1 piece of plastic canvas at least 4½" × 15½" for the bag bottom (available at craft and sewing stores)

* ⅝"-wide velvet ribbon for the rosettes: 1¼ yards of color 2, 1½ yards each of colors 1 and 3, and ¾ yard of color 4

* 1¾ yards of ⅝"-wide green velvet ribbon for the leaves and stem

* ¾ yard of 1"-wide ribbon trim for the outside pocket, side panels, and zipper tape lining

* Coordinating thread

* 18" zipper (non-separating)

* Zipper foot

* Appliqué glue

cutting

The pattern for the front and back panels is on pullout page P3.

Zipper placket / bag top:

* Cut 2 pieces 3″ × 19″ *each* from the zipper placket fabric, lining fabric, fleece, and interfacing.

* Cut 1 strip 3″ long from the ribbon trim for the end of the zipper inside lining.

Bag sides:

* Cut 2 pieces 5″ × 7″ *each* from the bag side fabric, lining fabric, fleece, and interfacing.

* Cut 2 strips 7″ long from the ribbon trim.

Bag front panel and back pocket:

* Cut 64 squares 2½″ × 2½″ from the print patchwork fabrics.

* Cut 1 pattern piece from the fusible fleece.

Bag back panel:

* Cut 1 pattern piece from the back panel fabric.

* Cut 1 pattern piece from the fusible fleece.

Bag bottom:

* Cut 1 piece 5″ × 16″ *each* from the bag bottom fabric, lining fabric, fleece, and interfacing.

* Cut 1 piece 4½″ × 15½″ from the plastic canvas.

Outside pocket:

* Cut 2 strips 8½″ × 2½″ from your fabric of choice for the pocket top band.

* Cut 1 piece 10½″ × 8½″ from the interfacing.

* Cut 1 strip 8½″ long from the ribbon trim.

Bag lining:

* Cut 2 pattern pieces *each* from the lining fabric and interfacing.

Inside pocket:

* Cut 1 piece 10½″ × 8½″ *each* from the lining fabric and interfacing.

Handles:

* Cut 2 strips 22″ × 3½″ *each* from the handle fabric and fleece.

Velvet ribbon:

* Color 1: Cut 2 strips ¾ yard long.

* Color 2: Cut 1 strip ¾ yard long and 1 strip ½ yard long.

* Color 3: Cut 2 strips ¾ yard long *each*.

* Color 4: Cut 1 strip ¾ yard long.

* Green: Cut a 9″ strip for the stem and 10 strips 5″ long *each* for the leaves.

See Sewing Basics on page 20. For extra zipper help, see Keeping It Real: A Common Zipper Boo-Boo and a Tip (page 51).

To account for the varying widths of zippers available, I've had you cut the zipper placket fabric slightly wider than you may need. After sewing the piece together, trim to exactly 5″ wide if needed, trimming equal amounts from each side. For example, if your zipper placket comes out to 6″ wide, trim ½″ off each side.

1. Fuse fleece to the wrong side of each placket piece. Fuse interfacing to the wrong side of each placket lining piece.

note: To insert the zipper, I am going to have you make a zipper "sandwich" with the outside and lining placket pieces you cut. You'll place the edges of the zipper between the lining and the outside fabric on either side and stitch to create a placket, which will also form the top of the bag.

2. Lay 1 lining piece right side up, and place the *closed* zipper right side up on top, so the zipper edge overlaps the fabric. Add a piece of the placket fabric, right side down, over the same zipper edge, with the edges of the fabrics lined up.

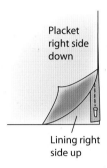

Placket right side down

Lining right side up

3. Pin the layers together carefully. Using a zipper foot, sew the layers together ¼″ from the zipper teeth, backstitching at each end.

Position of zipper between layers

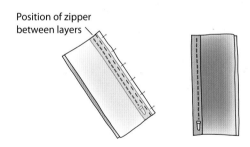

4. Repeat Steps 2 and 3 for the opposite side of the zipper placket. Press open and trim the placket fabric ends to within ½″ of the ends of the zipper if necessary.

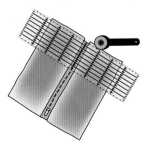

5. Fold the 3″ piece of ribbon trim in half crosswise, wrong sides together, and top-stitch the edges together. Sew the tab across the placket at the bottom of the zipper on the lining side.

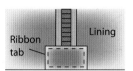

Ribbon tab

Lining

Keeping It Real

A Common Zipper Boo-Boo and a Tip

Be very careful to stitch at least ¼″ away from the zipper teeth. If you get too close, the fabric can get caught in the zipper when you open and close it.

Around the zipper pull, it often becomes difficult to sew. There are two things you can do to help with this. First, always keep your needle in the down position when you pause. When you come near the zipper pull, open the zipper so the pull is behind your needle.

Another trick, especially when you start stitching, is to manually stitch by rotating your machine's wheel a couple of rounds until you are past the difficult parts. Again, keeping your needle in the down position when you pause stitching will prevent the layers from shifting.

MAKE THE FRONT AND BACK PANELS

Create the patchwork

For tips on sewing patchwork, see Keeping It Real: Perfect Patchwork Piecing (page 58).

1. Randomly arrange your 2½″ patchwork fabric squares into 8 rows of 8 squares each.

2. Sew each row together, press, and then sew the 8 rows to each other. Press.

3. Lay the patchwork flat on a cutting mat and rotate it so the squares are on point.

4. Because you will cut both the front bag panel and the outside back pocket from the patchwork, leave enough room for the pocket when positioning the panel pattern. Using your cut lining piece as your pattern piece, align the center with the center of the patchwork, as close to the top as possible (as shown), and pin.

5. Line up a clear quilting ruler along the bottom edge of the pattern, and use a rotary cutter to cut off a triangular piece. Set it aside to make the pocket. Finish cutting out the front panel.

Make the outside pocket

1. Cut the patchwork triangle in half to create 2 triangles and rotate them so they form a square 8½″ × 8½″. Sew the triangles together and press.

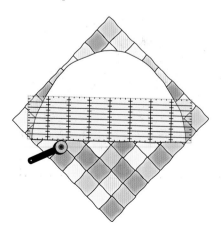

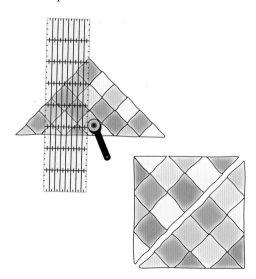

note: Here's where you will notice that the piece is a little small to make much of a pocket. To remedy this, you will add the 8½″ × 2½″ pieces of contrasting fabric.

2. Sew the fabric strips to the top and bottom edges of the patchwork square. Press.

3. Fuse interfacing to the wrong side of the pocket.

4. With the borders at the top and bottom, use chalk and a ruler to draw a horizontal line across the center of the pocket. Pin the ribbon trim across the pocket just below the center line. Fold the pocket in half to make sure the ribbon is just below the fold; adjust if needed. Sew both edges of the ribbon to the pocket.

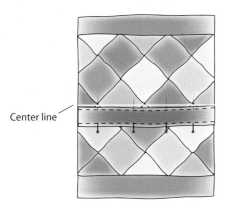

Center line

5. Fold the pocket in half with right sides facing and sew the side edges together. Trim the corners and press. Turn right side out and press again.

Finish the back panel

1. Fold the back panel piece in half to mark the center on the bottom edge. Do the same with the pocket you just made.

2. Align the raw edges of the pocket (with ribbon trim facing out) with the bottom edge of the panel, matching the center marks. Topstitch each side edge of the pocket in place ⅛″ from the edge. Backstitch at each end. At each top corner of the pocket, sew a ¼″ triangle to give the pocket extra support.

3. Measure 3″ from the right edge of the pocket and mark a vertical line with chalk, using a ruler. Stitch along the marked line, backstitching at each end, to create divided pockets.

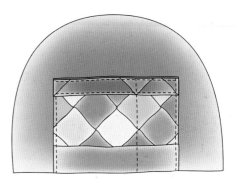

MAKE THE RIBBON ROSETTES AND
EMBELLISH THE BAG FRONT

note: As you attach these embellishments, be sure you steer clear of the bag front's seam allowances except for the bottom left stem, which can be sewn into the seam. Refer to the photo for placement.

1. Baste along the center of each piece of ribbon you cut for the flowers, and pull the top thread carefully to ruffle each piece.

2. Fold each piece of ribbon you cut for a leaf in half to form a flat "loop" with the velvet facing up. (It will look like a "cause" or "awareness" ribbon.) Overlap and tack the ends together with a touch of appliqué glue, then tack to the bag front.

3. At the sewing machine, create a flower on top of each leaf. Starting with an end of the ruffled ribbon in the center, begin topstitching the center of the ruffle, going around and around in circles until you have the desired size flower. Keep your needle in the down position so you can turn without shifting

the piece. Tuck the end under and stitch in place to finish.

4. Ruffle the stem portion and sew it in place. If you like, you can first attach it with a bit of appliqué glue.

Make 7 rosettes with leaves, sewing them to the patchwork bag front as shown in the photo. Make 3 extra leaves and tack them to the bag front at the lower left side of the flower arrangement.

MAKE AND ATTACH THE BAG HANDLES

1. Center and press the fusible fleece onto the wrong side of each handle strip.

2. Fold each handle in half lengthwise, right sides together, and press. Sew the long raw edges together. Turn and press with the seam in the center. Topstitch ⅛″ from the long edges of each handle.

3. Fold the front and back panels in half and mark the center top of each with a pin.

4. For both the front and back, mark 3″ to each side of the center top, and then mark 2″ below each of these marks for the handle placement. With the seam sides out and the handle hanging down, pin the raw handle edges in place at the marks and stitch ½″ from the ends.

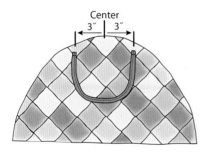

Fold the handle back up, covering the raw ends; stitch across the handle 1″ above the fold.

MAKE THE INSIDE POCKET

1. To make the lining pocket, follow the instructions for the outside patchwork pocket (page 52), eliminating the border strips and ribbon trim.

2. Topstitch the top of the pocket (at the fold) after you turn and press it for a decorative look and to hold the layers neatly together.

3. Sew the pocket to the front lining panel and stitch the divider as for the outside pocket.

CONSTRUCT THE BAG

Attach the bag sides to the zipper placket

1. Fuse the fleece to the wrong side of the outer fabric side panels, and fuse the interfacing to the wrong side of the lining side panels.

2. Attach the side panels to the ends of the zipper placket 1 side at a time, creating a "sandwich": Layer 1 side lining panel right side up, the zipper placket with the outer fabric right side up, and 1 outer fabric side panel wrong side up, as shown.

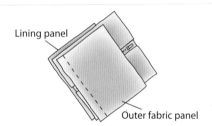

Lining panel

Outer fabric panel

3. Pin, then sew the raw edges together and press.

4. Press the assembled placket/side open. Pin the side lining piece back under the zipper placket to hold the lining out of the way. Sew ribbon trim along the top edge of the side outer fabric panel, stitching along both long edges of the trim. Unpin the lining.

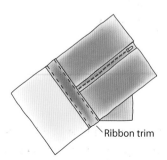

Ribbon trim

5. Repeat Steps 2–4 to add the remaining side panel.

Attach the front and back panels

note: I've had you make the side pieces extra long. This way, there's room for error if the front and back are not attached perfectly. You'll just need to trim the sides to match the front and back panels before you sew the bottom on.

1. Fuse the fleece to the wrong sides of the bag front and back outer fabric. Fuse the interfacing to the wrong sides of the bag front and back lining fabric.

2. Mark the center on the front and back panels and on the zipper placket/side panels. (Fold each in half to find the center and mark with a pin.)

3. Layer the front lining panel right side up, the zipper placket/side panels right side up (zipper pull faces up), and the front outside panel wrong side up. Sew the curved edges of the layers together. Clip the curves, turn, and press.

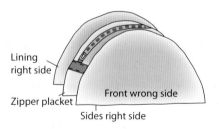

Lining right side

Zipper placket

Front wrong side

Sides right side

4. Repeat Step 3 to assemble the back, the remaining edge of the zipper placket, and the back lining panel.

Make and attach the bottom

1. Fuse the fleece to the wrong side of the bottom outer fabric. Fuse the interfacing to the wrong side of the bottom lining fabric.

2. Fold the bottom pieces in half and mark the center with a pin. Do the same for the front and back panel pieces.

3. Matching the centers, layer the bottom lining piece right side up, the front panel with the outer fabric right side up, and the outer bottom panel wrong side up. Sew the 3 layers together, starting and stopping ¼" from the ends; backstitch at both ends.

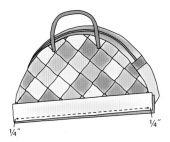

୧ **note:** In the next 2 steps you will just be sewing the outside bottom together. There will be 2 layers sewn together at this point instead of the 3 you were sewing together before.

4. Unzip the zipper and turn the bag wrong side out. Match the center of the outer bottom panel to the center of the outer back panel with right sides together. Sew the 2 layers together, starting and stopping ¼" from the ends; backstitch at both ends of the stitching.

5. With right sides together, pin the short ends of the outer bottom to the outer side panels. Sew the 2 layers together at each end, backstitching at both ends of the stitching.

6. Press the 3 unfinished edges of the bottom lining piece ¼" in toward the wrong side of the fabric.

7. Insert the plastic canvas bottom between the lining bottom and outside bottom pieces. Glue in place using fabric glue.

8. Whipstitch the bottom lining piece to the side panel and back panel lining pieces.

9. Press and turn the bag right side out. Press all of the seams again for a neat, crisp look.

Keeping It Real

Perfect Patchwork Piecing

If you're a beginning quilter, there are two really important things to know.

First: Make sure you always keep a consistent seam allowance. Getting a ¼″ foot for your machine makes this really easy.

Second: Press your rows properly so that intersecting seams will nest together neatly. For example, when you are piecing together rows of squares that need to match at the seams, press all the seams of Row 1 to the left, then press all the seams of Row 2 to the right. When you sew together the rows, right sides together, the seams will "nest."

As you match the seams together, feel the fabric and you'll notice there is a ridge where you pressed the seam of the top piece to one side and a ridge where you pressed the seam of the bottom piece to the other side. Butt these seams up to each other like a little puzzle fitting right into place, pin, and sew using a ¼″ seam allowance.

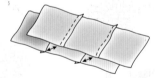

Press seams on adjacent pieces to opposite sides.

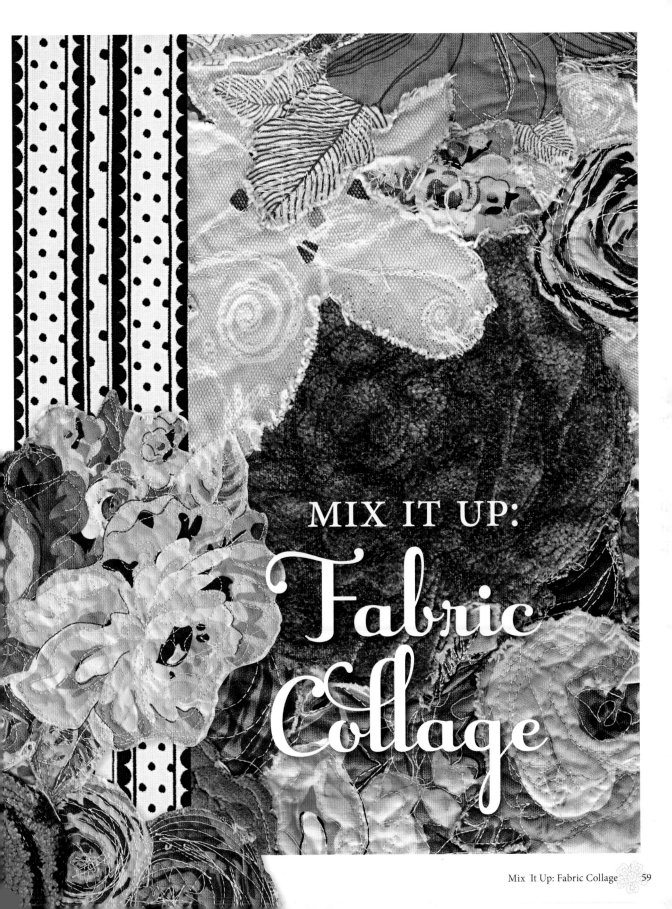

MIX IT UP:
Fabric Collage

Seasonal Wreath

FINISHED SIZE: 12″

If you haven't done fabric collage before, this simple project might be a good place to start. You can make this wreath for any season or occasion, depending on your choice of fabrics—florals for spring, hearts for Valentine's Day—anything you like.

You can make this wreath for any season or occasion.

For more on fabric collage, see Keeping It Real: Free-Motion Quilting and Fabric Collage (page 63). In addition to fabric collage, this project also involves stuffing various sections with polyester fiberfill for even more dimension and texture. A felt flower brooch adds the finishing touch. To make the brooch, see Flower Brooch (page 43).

materials

* 30 or more fabric scraps with floral motifs (or motifs to match the season)

* 1 fat quarter of muslin

* 1 fat quarter of coordinating fabric for the backing

* 1 fat quarter of thick wool batting

* Matching or contrasting thread for quilting

* Ribbon

* Small amount of polyester fiberfill

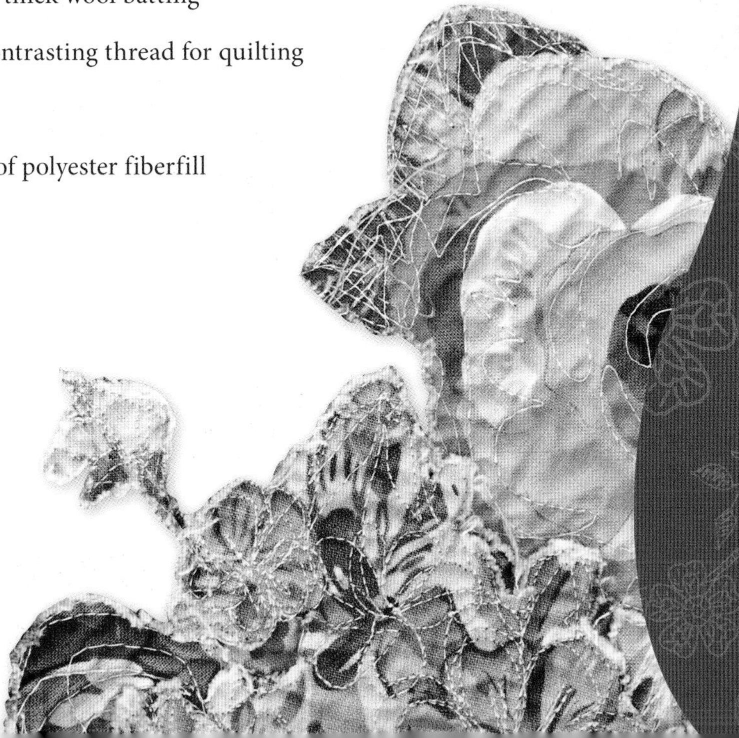

MAKE THE FABRIC COLLAGE

1. Layer materials on a flat surface with the backing on the bottom, wrong side up; the batting next; and the muslin on top.

2. Cut out floral motifs and arrange them in the shape of a wreath on top of the muslin. Pin each motif in place through all 3 layers, using plenty of pins.

3. Set up your machine for free-motion quilting and quilt the edge of a motif, leaving an opening to add a little bit of fiberfill.

4. Stuff the motif lightly. Quilt the edge of the motif closed, and then quilt on top of the motif.

5. Continue quilting motifs—some with fiberfill and some without—for a textured look.

FINISH THE WREATH

1. Cut away the excess fabric on the inside and outside of the wreath. Wet the entire piece and wring it out to add a wrinkled dimension. Allow it to air dry.

2. To finish the raw edges, sew a zigzag stitch around the edges of each motif 3 times, making the stitch shorter each time to achieve a satin-stitch finish.

Optional: Make a felt flower brooch and pin it to the wreath.

Keeping It Real

No Sticky Stuff!

It's not a good idea to use sticky stuff like fabric glue or fusible web to hold your cut motif pieces in place. Trust me on this one. I've attempted it. The sticky stuff often causes your sewing machine needle to catch and the tension to be altered, resulting in breaking thread and other problems. Use pins.

Keeping It Real

Free-Motion Quilting and Fabric Collage

One of my favorite sewing techniques is free-motion quilting used with fabric collage. For some time, I had been doing a variation on this technique by incorporating little scraps and using machine appliqué stitches to collage them together. And then I discovered free-motion quilting. A whole new world opened up.

Fabric collage uses free-motion quilting to create gorgeous fabric vignettes on quilts, clothing, pillows—pretty much anywhere you want to add a little flair. Motifs cut from a wide variety of large- and small-print fabrics are layered and then quilted together to create a usable piece of fabric art.

One thing I like is its instantly freeing nature. Using the free-motion quilting foot on your machine, with your feed dogs down, you simply doodle away using thread as your medium. You can trace the fabric motifs, add quilted leaves and flowers, even sign your name or throw in words and lines of poetry here and there.

There are no rules. Layer all kinds of fabrics together. I use everything from quilting cotton to lace and velvet to selvage edges, ribbon, and silk. I often cut out an appliqué shape rather than a fabric motif and throw that in the mix as well. Truly, anything goes. And you don't have to be overly concerned about your stitch lengths because when you are finished, you wet down the piece and allow it to dry, giving it a lovely worn look and hiding any "flaws."

Practice on scrap fabric to get used to it, and then—away you go! For some tips, see the following page.

* Use a free-motion foot (also called a darning foot), and drop the feed dogs so you can sew freely in every direction.

* Quilting gloves are wonderfully useful. They help you grip the fabric, and they keep your hands and wrists from becoming tired.

* Use tons of pins! The more the better. The last thing you want is flipping and flopping fabric pieces. When you have everything pinned down, pick up the piece and give it a good shake. Your pieces should all stay in place. Also, it's a good idea to use bright or white pins that contrast with your fabric. If you should end up with a pin sewn underneath a motif (I'll admit that I have—several times), don't panic. Just trim it out, place a new motif on top, and quilt it again.

* When I first started free-motion quilting, my instinct was to turn the fabric the way I would when I turned a corner doing appliqué. But I soon found I was working against myself by doing that. Simply move your fabric up, down, and side to side, gliding it underneath the needle gently.

* The back of your work is just as important as the front, so be sure to bring up the bobbin thread to the front before you start. Turn the wheel of your machine manually to make 1 stitch. Then raise the needle and wiggle the wheel a bit while gently tugging at the thread. You'll see the loop of the bobbin thread coming up. Pull it all the way to the front and continue sewing. Trim the threads on the top after several stitches to get them out of the way.

* Speaking of needles … just as when you are sewing a long distance, be sure that when you pause, you set your machine to the needle-down position to hold the fabric in place.

* You may need to play with the tension a bit to get it just right. Experiment on "practice" fabrics of the same weight as your project to adjust the tension.

* Stitch in 2 stages: First stitch the raw edges of all the pieces to get them attached so you can remove the pins. Then go back and do more decorative stitching to give the piece texture and depth.

* After quilting, wet down or wash the whole piece and hang it to dry or use your dryer. Washing allows the fabric to crinkle and gives you a nice, soft texture with frayed edges.

Flowering Container Garden Pillow

FINISHED SIZE: 23″ × 23″

Collage is even more fun when you use it to make something you can see and admire in your home. That's why I love this technique for all sorts of items. Really, who could bear to put a plain pillow anywhere again when you can have a pillow like this?

It gives a one-of-a-kind look to any space.

This design features a lavish collage of flower "blooms" in a bright, striped container. For detailed instructions on the fabric collage, see Keeping It Real: Free-Motion Quilting and Fabric Collage (page 63).

materials

* Approximately 72 floral motifs, in a variety of large and small prints, for the fabric collage

* 1 fat quarter of striped fabric for the flower container

* ¾ yard of contrasting background fabric*

* ¾ yard of fabric for the pillow back (I used denim.)

* 3 yards of ribbon for the pillow back ties

* 1½ yards of woven cotton fusible interfacing

* ½ yard of fusible fleece

* Coordinating or contrasting thread (I love variegated thread for collage.)

* 24″ × 24″ pillow form

*I'd suggest using something pretty subdued to allow for a nice contrast between the flowers and the background.

cutting

* Cut out the flower collage motifs as you compose your piece because that way you can balance the colors and sizes visually.

* Flower container fabric: Cut 1 of pattern A.

* Background fabric and fusible fleece: Cut 1 square *each* 23½″ × 23½″.

* Pillow back: Cut 2 pieces, *each* 23½″ × 16″.

* Woven cotton fusible interfacing: Cut 1 square 23½″ × 23½″ and 2 pieces 23½″ × 16″.

* Ribbon: Cut 4 pieces ¾ yard long *each*.

BUILD THE COLLAGE

1. Fuse interfacing to the wrong side of the background fabric.

2. Referring to the photo (page 65) and without pinning anything in place yet, lay the container piece at the bottom center of the background piece. Begin cutting out and layering flowers to fill and overflow the pot. Remember to mix larger- and smaller-scale pieces to balance your design, and remember to balance the color throughout the piece. If you notice a concentration of color in one area and none of that color in another area, you might want to move the pieces around. The same goes for large and small pieces.

3. Refer to Keeping It Real: Free-Motion Quilting and Fabric Collage (page 63) to pin, quilt, and finish your collage.

4. Press the fleece to the wrong side of the collage.

5. To round the pillow corners and prevent them from being pointy, place a bowl in a corner. Draw around the edge of the bowl at the corner. Cut along the marked line. Repeat for all 4 corners.

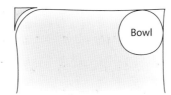

FINISH THE PILLOW

1. Follow the instructions in Keeping It Real: Making a Ribbon-Tied Pillow Back (page 69) to create the back and assemble the pillow.

2. Insert the pillow form through the back opening, fluff, and tie the pillow ties.

Keeping It Real

Making a Ribbon-Tied Pillow Back

This style of pillow back is pretty to look at, and it lets you remove the pillow form easily if you want to clean the pillow cover. I have you make this back for the Sweet Home Chicago Pillow (page 109) as well as the Flowering Container Garden Pillow. See Sewing Basics on page 20.

1. Fuse interfacing to the wrong sides of the pillow back pieces. On a long edge of each, turn under ¼″ and press, then turn another ¼″ and press. Stitch ⅛″ from the folded edge.

2. Place the 2 back pieces right side up on the wrong side of the pillow front, aligning and overlapping them to match the size of the pillow front. Pin the overlap together at the top and bottom edges (don't pin the back pieces to the pillow front yet). Baste the overlapping edges together ⅛″ from the top and bottom edges.

3. To mark the placement of the ribbon ties, measure and mark the center of the overlapping edges. Place the tie marks 4″ from the middle and 3″ back from where the pieces overlap. Fold an end of each piece of ribbon under ½″ and pin the ribbons in place as shown, with the folded raw edges tucked underneath.

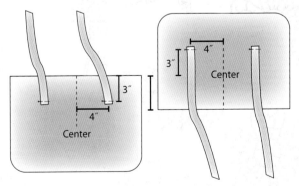

Note: Pieces shown side by side to show overlap. The two pieces are actually overlapped and basted together at the point.

4. Sew the ribbons in place and topstitch a rectangle with an X through the middle on the folded ends.

5. Pin the pillow front and back together with right sides facing and edges even. Cut the back corners to match the front corners. Sew together and press. Clip the rounded edges to—but not through— the stitching, and turn the pillow right side out.

TREE OF DREAMS

Wallhanging

FINISHED SIZE: 39″ × 66″

This project came about as an extension of the tree collages I was creating for my handbag line. I got to thinking these collages would be great wallhangings. Then I thought,

How about a giant wallhanging?

So, nearly life-sized, my "tree of dreams" emerged as a project for you. (See the complete wallhanging on page 72.) You'll be doing a lot of free-motion quilting on this project. For simple instructions, see Keeping It Real: Free-Motion Quilting and Fabric Collage (page 63).

materials

* Your favorite fabric scraps in floral and leaf motifs for the leaves, enough to cut 150 to 200 motifs*

* Fabric scraps about 6″ × 36″ with brown and green tones (preferably prints with a textured look) for the trunk

* Fabric scraps 6″–12″ × 44″ for the hill behind the tree

* ½ yard of green printed fabric for "grass" background

* 1½ yards of blue printed fabric for "sky" background

* 2 yards of muslin or flannel to be used in place of batting

* 2 yards of backing fabric

* ½ yard of fabric for binding

* 2 spools of thread to match your fabric

*It's fun to include textured velvets, silks, and corduroys. I even like putting tulle and lace on top of pieces. Also, don't be afraid to add in the random selvage or cut words from the selvage.

cutting

* From the binding fabric: Cut 6 strips 2¼″ × 42″.

* Cut the additional fabrics as you go.

Inspired to Sew by Bari J.

ASSEMBLE AND LAYER THE BACKGROUND

1. Use a rotary cutter and ruler to true up your green and blue background fabrics (make the bottom and top edges parallel and the side edges parallel while keeping 90° angles at the corners). Do the same with the muslin or flannel and the backing fabric.

2. Sew the top edge of the green "grass" fabric to the bottom edge of the blue "sky" fabric. Press. You can leave the selvages on for now; you'll cut these off later when you true up the whole piece.

3. On a large table or the floor, lay out the 3 layers with the backing right side down, the muslin or flannel next, and the background that you just sewed on top, right side up.

4. Align 1 of the long edges, and sew the 3 layers together just on that side. This will help keep the layers from slipping as you sew. Do not sew any other sides together; often this will result in lumps.

5. For the hill, cut curved pieces from the contrasting green print fabrics to layer on top of each other. Refer to the photo (page 72) to lay the pieces on top of the green grass with the hill rising to the side. Pin on securely, using many pins.

BUILD THE FABRIC COLLAGE

1. Now start with your free-motion quilting (page 63). Sew all the raw edges of the pieces now so they are attached and you can remove the pins. Later you will go back to do the decorative stitching.

2. Once you've got the hill pieces in place and attached well, lay the piece out flat again and start creating the trunk. Use your various green and brown fabrics to create a trunk effect. Just layer one on top of another until you have the look that you like. *To keep proportions correct, your trunk should go about ⅔ of the way to the top of the piece, with the rest reserved for leaves.* Pin the pieces in place securely. Quilt the trunk just to make it stable, and again wait to do the decorative stitching later.

Inspired to Sew by Bari J.

3. Cut various floral and leaf motifs to fill the branches of your tree. I cut around 150 to 200 or more pieces. Play with and arrange the motifs so the effect is pleasing to your eye. Pin the pieces securely and quilt to hold them in place.

4. Now go back and quilt all over your whole piece. Remember, free-motion quilting adds shading and texture to your art—you are giving the piece an added dimension that is not there with just the fabric.

5. When you've finished quilting to your liking, wet down or wash and dry the whole piece to crinkle the fabric and create a soft texture with frayed edges.

Keeping It Real

It's All About What *You* Like

"Pleasing to your eye." To some people that sounds scary. But this project is really all about what looks good to you. It's a collage—you can't go wrong. Imagine the leaves on a tree hanging down or swaying in the wind. Toward the outer leaves, you might want to create gaps the way a tree thins out toward the edges. The motifs hang down around the trunk; they have an active look.

When you are layering fabrics, don't fret about how it all looks at first. Just keep adding, mixing, and matching until you like the composition. You'll move and place things several times before it looks just right.

When choosing colors for the trunk and hill, try to pick tones that are similar but that have enough contrast so your leaves stand out from the trunk and the background.

Eventually it will all fall in place, just the way you want it to.

Keeping It Real

Free-Motion "Doodling Ideas"

On the grass portion of the wallhanging, use a back and forth motion to give it the look of grass. Doodle flowers coming up from the grass and trace the motifs in your fabrics. On the trunk, stitch up and down in rough, long ovals to mimic the texture of tree bark. In the leaves, you can trace motifs and stitch flowers and leaves on top of the tracing.

FINISH THE WALLHANGING

1. True up the edges of the piece as you did in the beginning, before you started sewing, cutting off the selvages. The trued edges should measure approximately 39″ × 66″. Bind the entire quilt, following the instructions in Keeping It Real: Binding Quilts and Other Sewn Projects (page 81).

2. Hand sew a rod sleeve to the back or see the Mini Memory Quilt (page 76) for optional hanging instructions.

ASSEMBLE THE PINWHEEL

1. Press the fusible web to the wrong side of 1 of the 6″ squares. Peel off the paper backing and press it to the wrong side of the other 6″ square to create a double-sided piece of fabric.

2. Using a quilting ruler and chalk or air erasable marker, draw diagonal lines from corner to corner of the square. Cut from each corner to 1″ before the center.

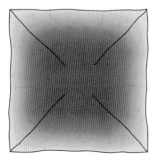

3. Bring a corner to the center and tack it in place with appliqué glue. Then bring its opposite corner to the center. Repeat for the other 2 corners.

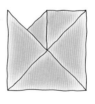

4. Set aside and allow the glue to dry while you construct the blocks.

CREATE THE PHOTO TRANSFERS

Use your selected family photos to create photo transfers. I do this using Printed Treasures, a lightweight fabric backed in paper that you use in your home computer printer. It is one of many brands, but it happens to be the one I like best. In this project it is used to print out your family photos on fabric. Follow the instructions on the package for best results.

MAKE THE BLOCKS

See Sewing Basics on page 20.

1. Sew the 4 block squares together in 2 rows of 2 squares each. Press.

2. Arrange your cut-out fabric motifs and photo transfer fabric pieces on the bottom right block.

3. Set up your machine for free-motion quilting and quilt the pieces in place. See Keeping It Real: Free-Motion Quilting and Fabric Collage (page 63) for instructions.

CREATE THE POCKETS

1. With right sides facing each other, sew the rectangular pocket pieces together, leaving a 2″ opening in the bottom.

2. Press your stitching and press the opening in toward the wrong side ¼″. Trim the corners, turn right side out, and press.

3. Place the pocket on the horizontal center of the bottom left square. Be sure it is slightly off center vertically, so that once you put photos and other goodies in it, they won't stick up into the top left block.

4. Pin and topstitch the side and bottom edges of the pocket in place using a ⅛″ seam allowance.

5. Create the rounded pocket in the same manner, following Steps 1–4 and sewing the pocket on the top right-hand block.

ADD THE FINISHING TOUCHES

1. Layer the backing, wrong side up, the flannel batting, and the quilt top, right side up, on a flat surface. Pin the layers together.

2. Follow the instructions on page 81 to bind the mini quilt.

3. Sew a button to the middle of the pinwheel, and sew the pinwheel to the center of the top left square.

4. To hang, sew the 3 plastic rings on the back of the quilt at the top left, top right, and top center. Either tie some ribbon on the rings or hang with picture hooks. Or cover a board or canvas with fabric and hang the mini quilt in the center—you could even frame it for an extra decorative touch.

Keeping It Real

Binding Quilts and Other Sewn Projects

These instructions are for double-fold binding.

1. Measure the perimeter of the piece you want to bind, and cut enough 2¼"-wide binding strips to equal the perimeter plus at least 14".

2. Sew the binding strips together end to end using diagonal seams. Trim as shown and press the seam to one side.

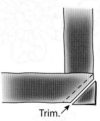

Trim.

3. Press the binding in half lengthwise, wrong sides together.

4. Working on the right side of the quilt top or other project, align the raw edges of the binding with the raw edges of the project piece, leaving at least a 6" tail. Begin sewing, starting in the center of one edge, using a ¼" seam allowance.

5. If you are binding a quilt or other project with 90° corners, you'll want to miter the binding corners. As you approach a corner, stop sewing and backstitch ¼" from the end. Clip the threads.

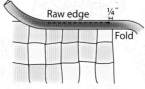

Raw edge   ¼"

Fold

6. Turn the quilt so that it's ready for you to sew the next side. Fold the binding strip away from you at a 90° angle to the side you just sewed. The point of the fold should be in alignment with the corner so the fold is at a 45° angle.

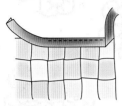

7. Fold the binding strip back down on itself, toward you, to create the mitered corner. Stitch from the end of the second edge again to ¼″ from the end of the side and repeat the mitering process at each corner. Repeat all steps for all sides of the project.

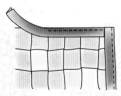

8. When you are approximately 12″ from where you started sewing on the binding, stop and backstitch. Open up a piece of the binding, fold the end in at a 45° angle, and trim it off to create a square piece. You will use this piece as a guide for how much the 2 ends should overlap.

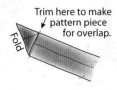

Trim here to make pattern piece for overlap.

Fold

9. Overlap the 2 ends and place the piece you cut as a guide over the 2 overlapping pieces. Trim both pieces so they overlap only for the length of the guide piece.

Make sure that when you overlap the 2 binding ends, you pull tightly to test that they fit. Don't test fit with the fabric sitting loosely, or you'll end up with too much fabric left over on the binding, causing a rippling effect.

Guide

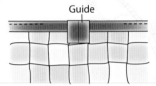

10. Open up the binding and place the ends at right angles to each other, right sides together. Using a ¼″ seam allowance, sew the 2 pieces together at a 45° angle.

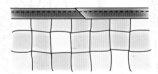

11. Continue sewing the binding to the quilt.

12. Wrap the binding to the back side and blindstitch it in place by hand. Press.

Quilt back

ARTFUL INSPIRATIONS

For Your
Home

CRAZY QUILT
Lampshade Slipcover

I have the most adorable vintage pot metal lamp in my studio, but its shade was in need of a facelift. Slipcovers on furniture are wonderful because we can change them with the seasons or when we change our decor. So rather than take the glue-it-down approach, I created a slipcover for my little lamp. And I made it with some of the many fabric scraps stashed in my studio baskets and drawers. You can do the same thing with your lamps. It's super-easy to make a pattern for any size shade.

This slipcover is made using crazy quilt patchwork piecing. It's fun and easy to do.

materials

* A cone-style lampshade (any size)

* 2 pieces of paper big enough to cover the lampshade all the way around (I used packing paper from a store that sells moving boxes.)

* Fabric scraps of any size, trimmed so the sides are straight

* 1 piece of muslin big enough to cover the lampshade

* Pom-pom trim or other trim to fit around the bottom edge of the lampshade

* Coordinating thread

CREATE THE PATTERN

1. Find the seam on the lampshade. Lay the shade on its side with the bottom of the seam at the bottom of the large piece of paper. Mark both ends of the seam on the paper.

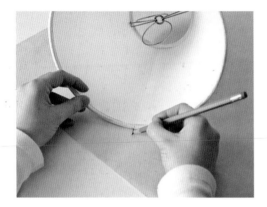

2. Roll the shade to the right, tracing its bottom curve with a pencil as you turn the shade. Stop at the seam and make a mark at the top and bottom of the seam.

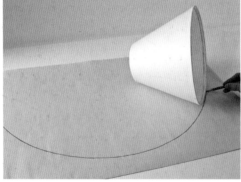

3. Roll the shade back to the starting point again, aligning the seam with the beginning seam marks. Be careful not to move the shade off your drawn line.

4. Repeat Steps 1–3 for the top edge of the lampshade.

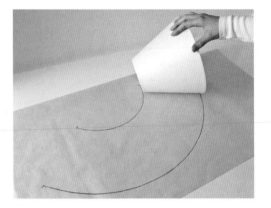

5. Using a ruler, draw lines to connect the top and bottom seam marks at each end. You now have an outline of the full shade.

6. To verify your measurements, measure the height of the lampshade to make sure it matches that of the outline all the way around. (Check each side first.) Using a tape measure, measure around the bottom and top of the lampshade, and make sure those match the length of the top and bottom lines you drew on the paper. Make any necessary adjustments.

7. Cut out the pattern piece, and wrap it around the shade to double-check that it matches.

8. Now add the seam allowances. Lay the pattern back down on another piece of paper. Using a ruler, make marks ½" outside the top edge and ¾" outside the bottom edge, and connect them. (Adding ¾" at the bottom gives you room for error: I'd rather my slipcover be a little bit long than find out at the end that it's too short.) Add ½" at both straight ends.

9. Discard the first pattern piece without seam allowances. Cut out the new pattern piece, and lay it on top of the piece of muslin. This will be your crazy piecing foundation.

To add the crazy quilt piecing, see Keeping It Real: Crazy Quilt It (page 88).

MAKE IT A SHADE

1. Place the finished crazy-quilted muslin piece on your cutting mat with the pattern piece on top, and cut out.

2. Match the 2 straight ends right sides together and pin. Using a scant ½" seam allowance, sew the 2 edges together. Press.

3. To hem the bottom edge, turn it to the wrong side ¼", press, and then turn it ¼" again and press. Pin and topstitch on the wrong side ⅛" from the edge of the hem. Repeat to hem the top edge.

4. Sew pom-pom or other trim to the bottom edge of the slipcover.

Keeping It Real

Crazy Quilt It

For this project, I'm going to show you how to crazy quilt with no raw edges showing rather than simply layering and topstitching fabric scraps as done on Jean Jacket Re-Vision (page 39). This technique is often referred to as "stitch and flip." Make sure the scraps you're using have straight edges.

Take your cut muslin to the sewing machine along with your straight-edged fabric scraps.

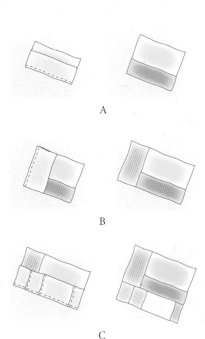

A

B

C

1. Place a scrap right side down in the middle of the muslin. Using a ¼″ seam allowance, sew an edge of the scrap to the muslin. Then flip it right side up with the seam underneath. Press. (A)

2. Place another scrap right side down on top of the piece you just sewed, with a long raw edge matching. Again using a ¼″ seam allowance, sew on the new piece, flip, and press. (B)

3. Continue adding pieces until the muslin is covered. You'll notice as you go that you need longer and longer strips. You can use long strips of a fabric, or you can create long strips by sewing together several pieces before you sew them to the muslin. You'll also see that angles are created as you go. Simply place the next strip farther back so when you flip it, it covers the odd angles. (C)

4. When finished, apply decorative stitches (on the sewing machine or by hand; I used my machine) on each of the seams for that vintage crazy quilt flair. You can go "crazy" here with your stitches and use many different types.

Tea Party Accessories

A luncheon at a lovely tearoom is one of my favorite things.

Not only do I adore those yummy scones and tea sandwiches, but I also love the atmosphere. The pretty napkins, the ladylike silverware, a sweet tea cozy—what could be better? With these adorable party accessories, you can create your own tearoom at home. Make teapot trivets, a tea cozy, and lovely lavender-scented "tea bag" sachet place cards. Spend an afternoon with your girlfriends, drink tea, indulge in a pastry—and when it's over, send your guests home with pretty teapot trivets and sachets made just for them.

Teapot Trivet

FINISHED SIZE: 14½″ × 6″

These dainty teapot trivets can be used as place settings and double as lovely party favors for your guests. Make them in a variety of fabrics tailored to each of your friends. These also make wonderful hostess gifts.

materials

Makes 1 teapot trivet.

* 1 piece 12" × 12" of print fabric for the base

* 4 pieces 7" × 8" of contrasting print fabric, 2 for the handle and 2 for the spout

* 2 pieces 4" × 12" of contrasting print for the lid

* 1 fat quarter of fusible fleece

* 1 piece 15" × 15" of heat-resistant batting, such as Insul-Bright

* Floral fabric scraps for embellishment

* 1 small button

* Coordinating thread for quilting

* Small amount of polyester fiberfill for the handle

* Air erasable marker or chalk

* Spray starch

cutting

Patterns are on pullout page P3. Cut pairs of pieces with right sides together.

* Base fabric: Cut 2 of pattern D on fold.

* Handle and spout fabric: Cut 2 *each* of patterns A and B.

* Lid fabric: Cut 2 of pattern C.

* Floral fabric scraps: Cut 5 circles in sizes graduating from 3½" down to 1½".

CREATE THE HANDLE

See Sewing Basics on page 20.

1. Sew the handle A pieces together, as shown, stopping at the notch on the inner curve, right sides together, and leaving the wide end open. Press. Clip the edges to—but not through—the stitching.

Notch.

2. Turn the piece and stuff lightly with fiberfill. Slipstitch the open seam closed using matching thread.

ASSEMBLE THE PIECES

1. Sew the straight edges of teapot lid C and teapot base D together. Repeat for the remaining lid and base pieces.

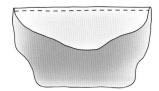

2. Press the stitches flat, and then press the seam up toward the teapot lid.

3. Sew spout B to the edge of 1 teapot base piece, on the right side of the fabric, as shown. The top of the spout base should be in line with the seam between the teapot base and lid.

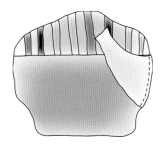

4. Press the stitches flat and then press the seam open.

5. Sew handle A to the opposite side of the teapot base from the spout, with the notched side toward the top. Press. Do not sew the remaining spout B in place yet.

6. Use the teapot panel without the spout and handle as a pattern to cut 2 matching pieces of fusible fleece and 1 piece of heat-resistant batting.

7. Press the fleece to the *wrong side* of each trivet panel.

8. Sew the remaining spout B in place, matching the placement of the first spout when the pieces are placed right sides together.

9. Place the 2 panels right sides together, and place the heat-resistant batting on top of one side. Pin well.

10. Leaving an opening at the bottom to turn, sew the pieces together. Press. Turn and press, pressing the opening edges under ¼″.

11. Edgestitch all the way around the piece ⅛″ from the edge. Backstitch at each end.

QUILT THE TRIVET

Using an air erasable marker or chalk and a ruler, mark a grid pattern on one side of the trivet. Start at the bottom left corner of the teapot base and mark lines 1″ apart all the way across at a 45° angle. Repeat, going the other direction, to create a grid pattern.

Topstitch the lines with coordinating thread, backstitching at the end of each line and trimming the threads. Alternate the stitching direction on each line to keep the fabric from warping. If you started from the right, do the next line from the left. Using a walking foot is also helpful.

EMBELLISH

1. To make the fabric flower, stack the 5 floral fabric circles right side up with the largest on the bottom and the smallest on top. Using a needle and thread, sew a gathering stitch in

a circle about ¼″–½″ from the center. Pull the ends of the thread to gather lightly.

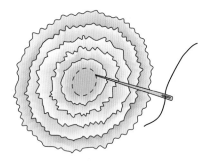

2. Wet the flower with spray starch and make it crinkly by pressing it dry with a hot iron. Create random creases and use your fingers to crunch, crinkle, and fray the edges a bit for a fun, rustic look.

3. Sew a button to the top center of the flower, and sew the piece onto your trivet at the top left corner near the handle.

Tea Cozy

FINISHED SIZE: 15½" × 9"

Create this cutie as a decorative embellishment for your table and to keep your tea nice and warm!

materials

* 1 fat quarter of print fabric for the tea cozy plus ⅛ yard for the binding

* ⅓ yard of contrasting print fabric for the lining, tab top, and scallop appliqués

* ¼ yard of double-sided fusible web, such as Wonder Under

* 1 fat quarter of fusible fleece

* Coordinating thread for quilting

cutting

Patterns are on pullout page P3.

* From the tea cozy fabric: Cut 2 of pattern A and 1 strip 35″ × 2¼″ for the binding.

* From the contrasting print fabric: Cut 1 piece 4″ × 2½″ for the tab top and 2 of pattern A for the lining. Set aside a piece large enough to cut 16 scallop pieces.

* From the fusible fleece: Cut 2 of pattern A.

MAKE THE SCALLOP APPLIQUÉS

These are raw-edge appliqués.

1. Press fusible web to the wrong side of a piece of the coordinating print fabric. Trace 16 of scallop pattern B and cut them out.

2. Remove the paper backing from the fusible web, and press 8 of the scallop appliqués along the bottom of each tea cozy panel.

3. Using a machine zigzag or blanket stitch, topstitch the raw edges of each scallop onto the panels.

MAKE THE TOP TAB

1. Fold the 4″ × 2½″ piece of fabric in half lengthwise, right sides together, and press. Sew the long raw edges together to create a tube. Press. Turn and press with the seam down the center of the back.

2. Edgestitch ⅛″ from each long edge of the tab. Fold the tab in half crosswise, with the seam facing in. Baste it to the center top of the right side of one outer panel, with the raw edges together and the fold facing down, using a ⅛″ seam allowance.

ASSEMBLE THE TEA COZY

1. Fuse the fleece to the wrong side of each cozy panel.

2. Sew the cozy panels together, right sides together, leaving the straight bottom edge open. Repeat for the lining panels.

3. Turn the cozy right side out. Place the lining inside the tea cozy with the wrong sides together, and pin at the seams.

4. Bind, following the instructions on page 81.

Optional: Add a floral embellishment to the top by following the instructions for Teapot Trivet (page 91).

Let lavender scent your table by using these tea bag sachets as a fresh take on place cards. These little treasures let you practice (or learn) a bit of hand embroidery. Your guest's initial on the tea bag tag personalizes each setting—and of course, it's another great party favor. A bowlful makes a lovely centerpiece, too.

materials

Makes 1 sachet.

* 1 piece of printed fabric 6″ × 3½″ for the sachet

* 2 tablespoons of dried lavender

* 1 piece of muslin big enough to fill a small embroidery hoop for the tag plus 1 piece 2″ × 3″ for the tag back

* Pinking shears

* Small scrap of felt for the leaf

* Coordinating pearl cotton embroidery thread

* Coordinating sewing thread

* Double-sided fusible web, such as Wonder Under

* Small button

* Small embroidery hoop

cutting

Patterns are on pullout page P3.

* From the felt, cut 1 of the leaf pattern B.

MAKE THE TAG

For information on basic embroidery stitches, see Keeping It Real: A Quick Guide to Hand Embroidery Stitches (page 101).

1. Trace the sachet tag pattern A on the center of the muslin in pencil or chalk, and write the initial of your choice in the middle of the traced piece.

2. Place the muslin in the embroidery hoop, stretched tight. With the pearl cotton, chainstitch the initial.

3. Press fusible web to the wrong side of an additional piece of muslin slightly larger than the tag.

4. Remove the muslin from the embroidery hoop and layer it on top of the second piece of muslin. Remove the paper from the fusible web and fuse the 2 tag pieces together. Cut out the tag shape, using pinking shears for the bottom edge.

5. Use pearl cotton to sew a running stitch about ⅛″ from the edges.

MAKE THE SACHET

See Sewing Basics on page 20.

1. Fold the piece of printed fabric in half crosswise with right sides together. Press. Sew the side edges together, leaving the top open.

2. At each bottom corner, clip to, but not through, the stitches. Press. Do not turn.

3. To make a box edge on the bottom of the tea bag, stand it straight up and fold a side seam down so the seam and bottom fold are aligned. Using a ¼″ seam allowance, sew across the tip of the triangle. Trim off the tip. Repeat for the opposite seam.

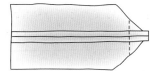

4. Turn the sachet right side out. Fold the side seams in toward the center of the bag and press to create a pleat on each side.

5. Fill the sachet ¾ full of lavender. Trim the top with pinking shears, fold the top down ¼″, and press in place. Stitch the sachet closed using a running stitch and pearl cotton.

EMBELLISH THE SACHET

1. Stitch the vein of the leaf using pearl cotton thread and a stem stitch.

2. Using the pearl cotton thread, sew the button onto the leaf and then onto the sachet. Do not cut the thread.

3. Extend the thread about 6″ and sew it to the tag to attach the tag to the bag.

Keeping It Real

A Quick Guide to Hand Embroidery Stitches

Embroidery is a great skill to learn—you can use it to embellish so many items, from garments to pillows. Here's a look at some basic stitches.

Running stitch | Bring thread up at 1 and down at 2, up at 3, and so on. Several stitches may be made at once by running the needle in and out of the fabric as shown.

Stem stitch | Bring the needle up at 1 and down at 2, up at 3, down at 4. Notice that each stitch begins halfway back by the previous stitch.

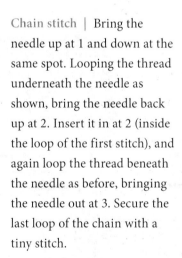

Chain stitch | Bring the needle up at 1 and down at the same spot. Looping the thread underneath the needle as shown, bring the needle back up at 2. Insert it in at 2 (inside the loop of the first stitch), and again loop the thread beneath the needle as before, bringing the needle out at 3. Secure the last loop of the chain with a tiny stitch.

To finish off your stitching | Bring the needle through to the wrong side of the fabric and weave it in along the back of the stitches for 1″–2″. Trim excess thread.

cutting

Patterns for the tree and the roof sides are on pullout page P2.

Cabin front and back walls:

* Cut 2 pieces 5″ × 4″ *each* from fabric and interfacing.

Cabin side walls:

* Cut 2 pieces 3½″ × 4″ *each* from fabric and interfacing.

Roof front and back:

* Cut 2 pieces 5″ × 3″ *each* from fabric and interfacing.

Roof sides:

* Cut 2 pattern A pieces *each* from fabric and interfacing.

Cabin bottom:

* Cut 1 piece 5″ × 3½″ *each* from fabric and interfacing.

Door appliqué:

* Cut 1 piece 1″ × 2″ from fabric.

Window appliqués:

* Cut 10 squares 1″ × 1″.

Tree appliqué:

* Cut 1 pattern B piece from fabric.

Needle book:

* Cut 1 piece 3½″ × 2½″ *each* from fabric and wool felt, using pinking shears to cut both at once with wrong sides together.

* Cut 1 strip 1″ × 2″ from fabric for button loop.

Sandbag:

* Cut 2 squares 3½″ × 3½″ from muslin.

MAKE THE CABIN WALLS

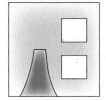

Left side

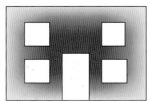

Front side

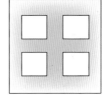

Right side

To prevent fraying and stabilize the fabric for quilting, press the interfacing pieces to the wrong sides of the wall, roof, and bottom pieces before you start sewing.

Cabin front

Cabin back with needle book

note: Position the front and back panels with the 5″ edges at the top and bottom.

1. Referring to the photo, use appliqué glue to adhere the windows and doors to the front panel.

2. Using your free-motion quilting foot and with the feed dogs down, sew on the door and windows. Using this method, you can simply doodle with your thread. Create window frame and door details, and add a scalloped edge ½″ from the top for an artful roofline.

1. To make the button loop, press each long edge of the 1″ × 2″ fabric strip under ¼″, then fold in half lengthwise with wrong sides together. Edgestitch the open edges together.

2. Layer the felt and cotton needle book fabrics with wrong sides together. Fold in half to form a book with the felt on the inside. Mark the center fold at the top and bottom with pins.

3. Fold the button loop in half and tack the ends together with glue. With the felt side of the book facing up, insert the loop ends between the layers in the center of the left edge. Beginning and ending at the center pin marks, topstitch around the left-hand side of the book, catching the loop ends in the stitching.

4. Fold the book in half again and center it on the cabin back. Beginning and ending at the center pins, topstitch the right-hand side of the book to the cabin back. Sew a button onto the cabin back to correspond with the loop for fastening the book closed.

Cabin sides

note: Position the cabin sides with the 3½″ edges at the top and bottom.

1. For the right-hand side of the cabin (when viewed from the front), glue windows in place and free-motion quilt as you did on the cabin front.

2. For the left-hand side of the cabin, glue and then free-motion quilt the tree trunk and the windows in place. Use green thread to add a mass of stitching for tree leaves. Then free-motion stitch with contrasting thread on top.

ASSEMBLE THE CABIN

See Sewing Basics on page 20.

Front, back, and sides

1. Mark a small dot ¼″ from each corner on the wrong side of all pieces. Use these dots as starting and ending points for each of your seams, and backstitch at each end.

2. Sew the top edges of the cabin front and cabin back pieces to the bottom edges of the roof pieces. Press the seams up. Sew the front and back together at the roof and press the seam to one side.

3. Sew the top edge of each cabin side to the bottom edge of 1 roof side piece A. Press the seams down.

☞ **note:** This is the opposite direction from the way you pressed the front and back seams. This is so you can easily sew the side to the front layer by nesting the seams.

4. With right sides together, align 1 side panel (cabin side and pattern A) to the front roof / wall panel that you constructed earlier. Nest the seams together. Sew the roof sides to the roof fronts and backs. Repeat for the remaining side.

5. Sew the front and back walls to the side walls. Press.

Sandbag

On such a large pincushion, you'll need something to weight the bottom down so it won't tilt. For this reason, I have you construct a sandbag.

1. Sew the muslin squares together, leaving a 1½″ opening to fill with sand.

2. Fill with sand or lizard litter and hand stitch the opening closed.

FINISH AND STUFF THE CABIN

1. Sew the bottom piece to 3 sides of the cabin, beginning and ending at the marked dots.

2. Turn the cabin right side out. Press the open bottom edges under ¼″.

3. Stuff the cabin firmly with fiberfill, and when it's nice and full, place the sandbag inside at the bottom. Before you close the seam, check to see if the house stands up straight. You will probably have to fiddle around with the placement of the sandbag to get it just right.

4. Hand stitch the opening closed using a blind stitch.

Sweet Home Chicago Collection

Having grown up in the suburbs just outside Chicago, I always dreamed of living "downtown." I especially wanted to live in the trendy Lincoln Park area of the city. And in my early 20s, that's what I did.

I loved living there among the beautiful row houses, with the park and zoo just a few blocks from my little studio apartment. Although I now live on the West Coast, the city of Chicago—with its historic and charming Lincoln Park—is my favorite place to visit, especially in the summertime. This quilt and pillow duo is my quilted tribute to my "sweet home" Chicago. Maybe it reminds you of a place near your sweet home.

SWEET HOME CHICAGO

FINISHED SIZE: 27″ × 13″ *Pillow*

materials

You can use a fun mix of prints for the row houses. Sometimes the fabric motifs add extra "architectural" details, as on the right-hand row house in the photo on page 108.

* ¼ yard or 1 fat quarter *each* of 6 coordinating fabrics for the row houses (fabrics A–F)

* ⅛ yard *each* of 3 or 4 blue fabrics for the sky (fabrics G, H, I)*

* ¼ yard of coordinating fabric for the border (fabric J)

* ¾ yard of coordinating fabric for the ruffle (fabric K)

* ⅞ yard of coordinating fabric for the pillow back

* ⅛ yard *each* of 3 colors of wool or wool blend felt for the window and door appliqués

* 5 yards of thin elastic cord for gathering the ruffle

* 1 yard of woven cotton fusible interfacing

* 2 yards of ribbon for the back ties

* 28″ × 14″ pillow form

* Appliqué glue

You'll be using the wrong side of the sky fabrics, so turn them over to see how you like them. Even prints that contain darker colors, such as brown, can work well.

Keeping It Real

Cutting Half-Square Triangles

There are several methods of cutting half-square triangles. In my directions I ask you to cut squares at 2⅞″. This is the most accurate way to get your squares to the correct finished size. You simply add ⅞″ to the desired finished measurement. However, many people round up to the next inch and trim after they sew the triangle. If you feel more confident doing it that way, by all means do so. But if you have a clear quilting ruler and a ¼″ foot on your sewing machine, you should have no problem using the ⅞″ measurement.

cutting

Appliqué patterns are on pullout pages P2 and P3.

note: Before you cut the squares for the half-square roof and sky triangles, see Keeping It Real: Cutting Half-Square Triangles (page 110).

Row houses:

* Cut 1 piece 4½″ × 6½″ and 2 squares 2⅞″ × 2⅞″ *each* from fabric A, fabric C, and fabric E.

* Cut 1 piece 4½″ × 8½″ from fabric B.

* Cut 1 piece 4½″ × 7½″ from fabric D.

* Cut 1 piece 4½″ × 5½″ from fabric F.

Sky:

* Cut 1 piece 4½″ × 1½″ and 4 squares 2⅞″ × 2⅞″ from fabric G.

* Cut 4 pieces 4½″ × 1½″ and 1 square 2⅞″ × 2⅞″ from fabric H.

* Cut 5 pieces 4½″ × 1½″ and 1 square 2⅞″ × 2⅞″ from fabric I.

Border:

* Cut 2 strips 2″ × 33″ and 2 strips 2″ × 20″ from fabric J.

Ruffle:

* Cut enough 4½″-wide strips from fabric K to total a minimum of 168″ when pieced together end to end.

Pillow back:

* Cut 2 pieces 27½″ × 11″ from the pillow back fabric.

Window and door appliqués:

From felt color 1:

* Cut 1 strip 1½″ × 6″; subcut into 2 rectangles 1½″ × 3″.

* Cut 1 strip 1″ × 10″; subcut into 10 squares 1″ × 1″.

* Cut 1 rectangle 1″ × 1½″.

* Cut 1 circle, pattern C.

* Cut 1 half circle, pattern HC.

From felt color 2:

* Cut 1 strip 1½″ × 6″; subcut into 2 rectangles 1½″ × 3″.

* Cut 1 strip 1″ × 11″; subcut into 11 squares 1″ × 1″.

* Cut 1 heart, pattern H.

From felt color 3:

* Cut 1 strip 1½″ × 6″; subcut into 2 rectangles 1½″ × 3″.

* Cut 1 strip 1″ × 8″; subcut into 8 squares 1″ × 1″.

* Cut 2 circles, pattern C.

* Cut 1 half circle, pattern HC.

Interfacing:

* Cut 1 piece 27½″ × 13½″ for the row houses.

* Cut 2 pieces 27½″ × 10″ for the pillow back.

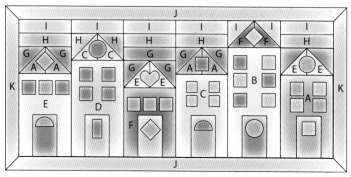

Assembly diagram

Make the roof/sky triangles

⌒ **note:** To create a faded look for the sky pieces and for maximum contrast between the roofs and the sky, use the wrong side of the sky fabrics. Also see Sewing Basics on page 20.

1. You will make 6 sets of 4 triangles, 1 for each row house roof. Refer to the assembly diagram to see which fabrics to use.

2. To create a set of 4 triangles, sandwich the *right side* of a roof square to the *wrong side* of a sky square.

3. Using a quilting ruler and either chalk or an air erasable marker, draw a line from a corner to its opposite corner on a diagonal. Then draw a line ¼″ to each side of the diagonal line.

4. Stitch on the 2 outer lines and cut the square in half along the middle line. You now have 2 pieced squares made of 2 triangles each. Repeat to make 6 sets, keeping the sets paired together.

5. You can either press seams toward the darker fabric so the seam doesn't show through or press 1 seam of each square in each direction, which is what I like to do. I find it easier to piece the squares together this way in the next step.

6. To complete a roof, layer 2 corresponding roof pieces, right sides together, with the raw edges of the roof fabrics aligned. Make sure the seams are matched up, and pin in place.

7. Using a ¼″ seam allowance, sew the raw edges of the roof triangles together. Press the seam to one side. Repeat for the remaining 5 roofs.

Attach the roofs to the houses

1. Sew each roof to its row house. Then sew the 4½″ × 1½″ sky pieces above the roofs, following the assembly diagram on page 112. Press the seams of the row house/sky sets in alternating directions—one up and the next down.

2. Sew the 6 row house/sky sets together, making sure the seams match as indicated in the diagram.

note: To avoid a warp in the fabric, stitch the seams between the row houses in opposite directions. So if you sew the first row house from top to bottom, flip the pieces over and sew the next seam from bottom to top.

MAKE THE BORDER

The contrasting border for this pillow is mitered at the corners like a picture frame. For general instructions, see Keeping It Real: Making A Mitered Border (page 115).

Appliqué the windows and doors

1. Press the 27½″ × 13½″ piece of interfacing to the wrong side of the assembled row house panel, with borders.

2. Using appliqué glue and referring to the assembly diagram (page 112), glue the felt pieces to the houses.

3. Stitch each felt piece in place with a hand or machine blanket stitch. I used contrasting thread for each. You can do the same or use matching thread.

4. To create panes on the windows, stitch across the centers horizontally and vertically, using a tiny zigzag stitch.

G note: I have found that if I sew a long strip on from end to end, often I'll have an extra ¼″ or so left over. To remedy this, I have made it a habit to mark the centers and sew from the center to an edge and then sew from the center to the other edge. This way I always end up with equal amounts of fabric on each side. And if for some reason I'm a tiny bit short, I can always give a little stretch to the offending piece.

6. Place the pillow or quilt with attached borders right side up on a cutting mat. Fold it in half diagonally so the right-hand border seam is aligned over the top border seam. Pin at the pivot point so it does not shift.

7. Take your quilting ruler and lay the 45° line along the stitches you just sewed. Make sure the 45° mark is facing you; otherwise your cutting line will be upside down. Align the edge of the ruler so it is ¼″ past your marked pivot point, being careful to keep that 45° line right on the seams. The edge of the ruler is your cutting line, and your sewing line is ¼″ inside that line. With a rotary cutter, carefully trim off the excess fabric at the cutting line.

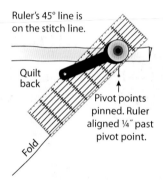

Ruler's 45° line is on the stitch line.

Quilt back

Fold

Pivot points pinned. Ruler aligned ¼″ past pivot point.

8. Pin the edge neatly in place just as you cut it, with *right* sides together. Using a ¼″ seam allowance, sew from the raw edge to the pivot point, backstitching at both ends.

Quilt back

Fold

9. Repeat Steps 6–8 on the other 3 corners. Open the miters and press the seams open.

SWEET HOME CHICAGO

FINISHED SIZE: 40″ × 56″ Quilt

materials

* ⅓ yard or 1 fat quarter *each* of 8 coordinating prints for the row houses and small park center squares (fabrics A–H)

* ⅛ yard *each* of 4 blue prints for the sky (fabrics I to L)*

* ⅓ yard *each* of 6 print fabrics for the park center and the tree appliqués (fabrics M–R)

* ¼ yard of contrasting felt for the top and bottom park borders

* ⅛ yard *each* of 3 colors of wool or wool blend felt for the window, door, bicycle, wagon, and flower cart appliqués

* ⅛ yard *each* of 2 shades of brown wool or wool blend felt for the puppy and squirrel appliqués and the flower cart appliqué

* 1⅞ yards of contrasting fabric for the quilt border (With this amount, there is no piecing.)

* 2¼ yards of contrasting fabric at least 42″ wide for the quilt backing

* 1¼ yards of contrasting fabric for a ruffle and ½ yard contrasting fabric for facing *or* ½ yard of contrasting fabric for a binding

* 3 yards of woven cotton fusible interfacing

* 1 yard of tearaway stabilizer for the appliqués

* Quilt batting, 44″ × 60″

* Freezer paper

* 13 yards of elastic cord for gathering ruffle (*optional*)

You'll be using the wrong side of the sky fabrics, so turn them over to see how you like them. Even prints with darker colors, such as brown, work well.

cutting

Appliqué patterns are on pullout pages P1–P3.

note: Before you cut the squares for the half-square roof and sky triangles, see Keeping It Real: Cutting Half-Square Triangles (page 110).

Row houses:

* Cut 2 pieces 4½″ × 6½″ and 4 squares 2⅞″ × 2⅞″ from fabric A.

* Cut 2 pieces 4½″ × 8½″ and 4 squares 2⅞″ × 2⅞″ from fabric B.

* Cut 2 pieces 4½″ × 6½″ and 4 squares 2⅞″ × 2⅞″ from fabric C.

* Cut 2 pieces 4½″ × 7½″ and 4 squares 2⅞″ × 2⅞″ from fabric D.

* Cut 2 pieces 4½″ × 6½″ from fabric E.

* Cut 2 pieces 4½″ × 5½″ from fabric F.

* Cut 2 pieces 4½″ × 7½″ from fabric G.

* Cut 2 pieces 4½″ × 5½″ from fabric H.

Sky:

* Cut 8 squares 2⅞″ × 2⅞″ from fabric I.

* Cut 6 pieces 4½″ × 1½″ and 6 squares 2⅞″ × 2⅞″ from fabric J.

* Cut 8 pieces 4½″ × 1½″ from fabric K.

* Cut 14 pieces 4½″ × 1½″ and 2 squares 2⅞″ × 2⅞″ from fabric L.

Park center:

* Cut 8 squares 4½″ × 4½″ from fabrics A–H (1 square from each fabric).

* Cut 10 squares 8½″ × 8½″ from fabrics M–R (1–3 squares from each fabric).

Top and bottom park borders:

* Cut 2 strips 2½″ × 32½″ from contrasting felt.

Border:

* Cut 2 strips 38″ × 4½″ and 2 strips 60″ × 4½″ from the border fabric.

Window and door appliqués:

From felt color 1:

* Cut 1 strip 18″ × 1½″; subcut into 6 pieces 1½″ × 3″.

* Cut 1 strip 1″ × 32″; subcut into 32 pieces 1″ × 1″.

* Cut 2 circles, pattern C.

* Cut 3 half-circles, pattern HC.

From felt color 2:

* Cut 1 strip 12″ × 1½″; subcut into 4 rectangles 1½″ × 3″.

* Cut 1 strip 28″ × 1″; subcut into 28 squares 1″ × 1″.

* Cut 4 circles, pattern C.

* Cut 3 half-circles, pattern HC.

From felt color 3:

* Cut 1 strip 18″ × 1½″; subcut into 6 pieces 1½″ × 3.

* Cut 1 strip 1″ × 20″; subcut into 20 squares 1″ × 1″.

* Cut 2 circles, pattern C.

* Cut 2 hearts, pattern H.

Tree, bicycle, and other appliqués:

* See Make the Appliqués (page 122).

Quilt backing:

* Cut 1 piece width of fabric × 60″.

Ruffle and facing (as shown):

* Cut 10 strips 4″ × 44″ from the ruffle fabric.

* Cut 5 strips 2½″ × 44″ from the contrasting fabric of your choice for the facing.

    or

Binding (*optional*):

* Cut 5 strips 2¼″ × 44″ from the binding fabric.

MAKE THE ROW HOUSES

To make the row houses with window and door appliqués, refer to the assembly diagram (at left) and the instructions for the Sweet Home Chicago Pillow (pages 109–116). Note that for the quilt, you will create 2 panels of row houses—1 for the top of the quilt and 1 for the bottom.

◟**note:** For all machine appliqué, use tear-away stabilizer underneath the fabric on the *wrong side*.

Assembly diagram

MAKE THE PARK CENTER

Sew together the pieces cut from the 6 park center fabrics, referring to the assembly diagram (page 121). Piece together the 4 sets of 4½″ × 4½″ squares first; then piece them to their coordinating rows and piece the rows together.

ATTACH THE PARK CENTER TOP AND BOTTOM BORDERS

1. Fold the park center in half vertically to find the center, and mark the top and bottom centers with a pin. Do the same with the felt border pieces.

2. Match the border pieces with the park center top and bottom edges, right sides together, and pin in place. Sew the borders to the park center, stitching from the center to the edge in each direction.

ATTACH THE HOUSE PANELS

1. Fold the row house panels in half vertically to find the centers and mark with a pin on each side.

2. Match the panels with the felt borders and sew in place, stitching from the center to the edge in each direction.

ATTACH THE QUILT BORDERS

1. Sew the short border strips to the top and bottom of the quilt. Trim the edges even with the quilt sides.

2. Sew the long border strips to the side edges of the quilt. Trim the ends even with the top and bottom edges of the quilt.

MAKE THE APPLIQUÉS

Appliqué patterns are on pullout pages P1–P3.

Tree appliqués

You will need 5 of tree pattern T1 and 5 of tree pattern T2. These appliqués, which are cut from cotton fabric, are made with edges turned under using the freezer paper appliqué method. For instructions, see Keeping It Real: Freezer Paper Appliqué (page 124). Refer to the assembly diagram for placement.

Bicycle, squirrel, puppy, wagon, and French market cart appliqués

Trace the pattern pieces from the pullout page and cut them from the wool felt fabrics. You will need 2 (reverse 1 set) of each squirrel pattern piece, 3 (reverse 1 set) of each puppy pattern piece, and 1 each of the other pattern pieces.

Use appliqué glue to place them, referring to the assembly diagram, and machine or hand appliqué them as you did the windows and doors (see page 113).

FINISHING

Make a quilt "sandwich." Lay the quilt backing flat, wrong side up, smooth the batting on top, and lay the quilt top, right side up, on top. Hand baste the layers together using long stitches, or pin at close intervals with safety pins.

Do the quilting

I had my quilt professionally quilted on a longarm quilt machine, but if you wish, you can quilt it on your home machine. For more information on quilting, consult a good basic book such as *Show Me How to Machine Quilt* by Kathy Sandbach or *Foolproof Machine Quilting* by Mary Mashuta, both available from C&T Publishing.

Bind the quilt or add a ruffle

If you want to bind your quilt, refer to the directions in Keeping It Real: Binding Quilts and Other Sewn Projects (page 81).

To make a ruffle, piece the ruffle strips together using ¼" seam allowances. Once the ruffle is attached, you will add a facing strip to finish the edge.

1. Sew together the ruffle strips in a continuous circle and create a ruffle using a ruffler foot or elastic cord as for the Sweet Home Chicago Pillow (page 114).

2. Fold the ruffle strip in half and mark the center of each side with a pin. Fold the quilt in half vertically and mark the center of the top and the bottom with a pin.

3. On the *right side* of the quilt, match the centers of the ruffle to the centers of the top and bottom with raw edges aligned. Distribute the ruffle evenly to each corner on the top and the bottom, and pin the raw edges in place.

4. Distribute the fabric evenly by pinning between each corner and the center of each side that you just pinned in place. Continue pinning the center between pins until you have the ruffle evenly distributed across each side.

5. Sew the ruffle onto the quilt, using a scant ¼" seam allowance. Press the stitching. Do not press the ruffle away from the quilt until the facing has been applied.

Create and attach a facing strip

1. Sew the short ends of the facing strips together and press.

2. With the quilt right side up, start at the center bottom edge and pin the facing strip right side down around the edges. *The quilt, ruffle, and facing raw edges should all be even.* Turn under and overlap the facing short ends.

3. Sew the facing in place using a ¼" seam allowance. Trim the corners. Press the facing to the back of the quilt and the ruffle away from the quilt.

4. Turn the facing raw edge under and hand stitch in place.

Keeping It Real

Freezer Paper Appliqué

For appliqué pieces with edges neatly turned under, try the freezer paper method. You can use it to apply appliqués to everything from quilts to garments. The cool thing about freezer paper is that the shiny side adheres to fabric and paper when pressed. Even better, it peels off easily and leaves behind no residue.

For this process, you'll need freezer paper, appliqué glue, spray starch, a stiletto tool, a small paintbrush, and an ultra-fine black permanent marker. I also recommend a mini iron for pressing under the edges. For more on these supplies, see page 13.

1. Trace your appliqué pattern piece with the marker onto the *shiny side* of the freezer paper.

2. Iron 3 pieces of paper on top of the *matte side* of the piece you just traced on. This creates a nice stiff template to work with.

3. Cut out the shape with your paper scissors.

4. Iron the *wrong side* of a piece of fabric at least ½″ larger than the template to the shiny side of your freezer paper template.

5. Cut the fabric around your template, leaving ¼″ to turn under.

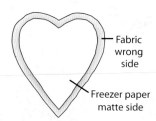

Fabric wrong side

Freezer paper matte side

6. Place the cut appliqué piece, right side down, on an ironing surface. Use a pin or 2 to tack it in place.

7. Spray a large amount of spray starch into a cup so that you have a good amount of liquid to dip in. Dip your paintbrush into the starch and paint a generous amount onto the ¼″ of extra fabric.

8. Using your stiletto tool, turn the wet, starched ¼″ allowance of fabric onto the matte side of the freezer paper, ironing as you go along.

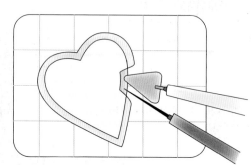

note: As you turn the fabric, get past tricky parts like the V of a heart by clipping with small scissors just barely to the freezer paper.

9. Carefully pull the paper out from the middle, and finger press or iron the turned fabric neatly in place.

10. Put tiny dabs of appliqué glue along the turned-under edge, and place the piece on your appliqué surface.

11. Let it set for a minute, and then blindstitch the piece in place by hand or machine appliqué.

Resources

ONLINE FABRIC AND NOTION STORES

Fabritopia
www.fabritopia.com
Carries a great selection of quilting fabrics, magazines, patterns, and books.

Fat Quarter Shop
www.fatquartershop.com
Carries a wide selection of quilting fabrics, notions, quilt kits, and more.

ONLINE AND BRICK-AND-MORTAR CRAFT STORES

Britex Fabrics
www.britexfabrics.com
146 Geary Street
San Francisco, CA 94108
415-392-2910

Out-of-this-world selection of fabrics and the largest collection of ribbons and trims I've ever seen in one place.

Dick Blick Art Materials
www.dickblick.com

The Fabric Depot
www.fabricdepot.com
700 SE 122nd Avenue
Portland, OR 97233
503-252-9530

Carries a large array of quilting fabrics, interfacings, notions, books, patterns, and more, as well as Form-Flex.

Hancocks of Paducah
www.hancocks-paducah.com
3841 Hinkleville Road
Paducah, KY 42001
(U.S.) 1-800-845-8723
(International) 1-270-443-4410

The famous Hancocks of Paducah carries fabric of all kinds, notions, supplies, books, patterns, and more.

Hobby Lobby
www.hobbylobby.com

Jo-Ann Fabric & Craft Stores
www.joann.com

Michaels Stores, Inc.
www.michaels.com

Vogue Fabrics
www.voguefabricsstore.com
718-732 Main Street
Evanston, IL 60602
847-864-9600

Renowned Chicago fabric store that stocks thousands of bolts of everything from silk to muslin. Also carries trim, notions, and pretty much anything else you can think of.

About the Author

Bari J. Ackerman is a product and textile designer living in the San Francisco Bay Area. Her work has been featured in such publications as *Sew Somerset, Romantic Homes, Haute Handbags,* and many more. She lives with her husband, Kevin, and two daughters, Anna and Emily. To find out more about Bari, visit her blog at www.barij.typepad.com or her website at www.barijonline.com.

For a list of other fine books from C&T Publishing, visit our website to view our catalog online:

C&T PUBLISHING, INC.

P.O. Box 1456
Lafayette, CA 94549
800-284-1114

Email: ctinfo@ctpub.com
Website: www.ctpub.com

C&T Publishing's professional photography services are now available to the public. Visit us at www.ctmediaservices.com.

Tips and Techniques can be found at www.ctpub.com > Consumer Resources > Quiltmaking Basics: Tips & Techniques for Quiltmaking & More

For quilting supplies:

COTTON PATCH

1025 Brown Ave.
Lafayette, CA 94549
Store: 925-284-1177
Mail order: 925-283-7883

Email: CottonPa@aol.com
Website: www.quiltusa.com

Note: Fabrics used in the quilts shown may not be currently available, as fabric manufacturers keep most fabrics in print for only a short time.